AN
ENCYCLOPEDIA
OF
SOFAS

AN
ENCYCLOPEDIA
OF
SOFAS

CONSTANCE KING

A QUANTUM BOOK

Published by Grange Books
An imprint of Grange Books plc
The Grange
Grange Yard
London SE1 3AG

ISBN 1-85627-862-X

Printed in Hong Kong by Sing Cheong Printing Co. Ltd

CONTENTS

Introduction   6

Before 1700   8

1700–1800   16

1800–1900   48

1900–1999   86

Chronology   120

Glossary   122

Explanatory Diagrams   124

Index   126

INTRODUCTION

Whether warm and companionable or coolly aloof and solitary, the sofa has assumed many guises over the years – and continues to do so. What can be more elegant than the simple lines of a Regency design, especially made to display the grace of a woman wearing a fashionable gauze dress? Or more comfortable and intimate than the feather-filled cushions of an Edwardian embossed-velvet settee with its atmosphere of opulence and comfort? As the sofa is such a large piece of furniture, it inevitably has been one of the focal points of a room's decorative scheme, and so has reflected in its development the influence of current fashions.

Since the 18th century, furniture historians have used various, and at times contradictory, terms to describe this item. The words settle, settee, sofa, couch, divan and even day-bed have often described almost identical objects. Occasionally there is some attempt to differentiate, one expert, for instance, suggesting that a sofa is to recline on, whereas a settee is intended for sitting upright. Other sources indicate that a sofa is used by only one person but a settee by several. To some a settle is a long wooden seat, to others it can have webbing or even springs. Some types have traditional terms that are in general use such as Knole, a Chesterfield or a chaise longue, but even these tend to be used loosely, one man's *conversation* being another's *indiscret*. For the purpose of this book, the general term 'sofa' is used to encompass a broad spectrum of diverse seat furniture, from an Egyptian style day-bed, to a chair-backed hall seat to a formal structure in the Biedermeier manner.

All sofas, because of their size, were relatively expensive items, their construction relying upon good-quality hardwood that was necessary for strength. The costliest versions, in all periods, were those with detailed carving or inlay (indeed, it was only in the 20th century that the cult of expensive simplicity and functionalism developed). Drawing-room sofas are, traditionally, display pieces, evidencing the taste and wealth of the householder. Consequently the upholstery fabric was of prime importance and sometimes even more expensive than the frame. If fine materials, such as silk, were used for covers, they had to be laid over a heavy lining fabric that would take some of the strain, and this again added to the cost. When braids, fringes and tassels were popular, many of the most extravagant trimmings were produced in France, but these were so costly that they were only used by the most exclusive furniture makers.

Throughout its history, the sofa has mirrored the social attitudes and etiquette of its country of origin. Those made in Germany tend to have rather high seats, because the sofa was positioned behind a table in middle-class homes. Symmetrical, rather plain designs were preferred, as the mistress of the house sat at one end and the most important visitor at the other – a formality that was observed on all occasions. In contrast, French interiors were much less restrained and sofas were grouped informally around the salon.

Many British and American mid-Victorian sofas, although large enough to seat several people, were only comfortable when used by one. In such pieces it was only the centre of the back that was fully padded, with the sides so heavily carved that they formed the most painful of back supports. Such sofas, with all the decoration rising to a crescendo in the middle, were superb fashion accessories for the crinoline-clad ladies of the 1850s and 1860s, and provided an excellent setting for receiving visitors. As behaviour became less formal and women abandoned the tightly laced corsets that forced them to sit upright, this relaxed attitude was reflected in the design of sofas, so much so that by 1900 there were feather-filled cushions and low seats.

From the 1840s, when sprung seats came into general use, writers on deportment tended to grumble about the lounging attitudes of men, who were often seen sprawling on sofas – even in the presence of ladies. Such complaints were even more vociferous in the early 20th century, when the low designs encouraged people to relax completely. By the 1920s, the arms on many sofas were broad enough to be used as side tables and some designs included wooden or glass inserts suitable for an ashtray or a cup of coffee. Such luxurious designs are seen at their most extreme in the Hollywood interiors of the 1930s.

Today, there is a considerable divergence between the adventurous work of the artist-designer, seen in exhibitions and in a few exclusive shops, and the every-day, commercial products, whose basic shapes have changed very little since the 1930s. There are even firms specializing in the manufacture of reproduction pieces, some of which are so complex that they can cost more than the 18th- or 19th-century originals.

In general, there are not many fakes in the antique-sofa market, because the cost of reproducing some of the more extreme designs has been – and is – far too prohibitive. Sofas that do not have any show-wood, such as Chesterfields, are more of a problem, as a reupholstered antique version does not look much different from a reproduction.

BEFORE

1700

Despite the relative simplicity of their tools, craftsmen of the ancient Egyptian and Greek civilizations created day-beds and sofas whose designs have provided furniture makers through the ages with the most elegant of basic forms. Very little actual furniture from Pharaonic Egypt and ancient Greece has survived, however; what knowledge there is mainly derives from murals and vase-paintings. Fortunately, the Egyptian custom of burying the dead with their possessions (for use in the afterlife) has provided a sufficient number of actual examples to enable some assessment to be made of this princely furniture.

The best-known collection was discovered near Luxor in 1922, in the tomb of Tutankhamen, who died c1350 BC. His golden throne, with lion-paw feet, exhibits a skilled use of inlay using precious stones, as well as the application of gold foil. Bull's feet were used on furniture in the First Dynasty (c3000 BC) but by the New Kingdom (c1567–1070 BC) the lion-foot form had become more popular, as shown by the funerary couches found in Tutankhamen's tomb. In an inlaid scene on the back of his gilded throne, the king is shown seated on an upholstered chair, suggesting that the craft of padded upholstery had its beginnings in Egypt.

Both couches and chairs were the province of the wealthy in ancient Egypt; ordinary people would have owned only the simplest items, such as wooden coffers and stools. Most of these couches seem to have been low and sloped down to the foot, but those used by Tutankhamen were very high, perhaps an indication of his rank. Both cushions and linen covers appeared on couches, although the double benches that seated a man and his wife in tomb reliefs were left plain. Veneers, marquetry and inlay were also used by the Egyptians.

In ancient Greece, couches used for eating as well as for reclining on during the day were status symbols. As with Pharaonic furniture, most knowledge of the design of Greek furniture is based not on surviving examples but on representations seen on vase-paintings and in small models. At first Egyptian-style animal legs continued to be popular, but these were gradually replaced by rectangular legs that were sometimes extended to hold a mattress or pillow in position. Some of the scroll couches with scroll-decorated pillow rests were wide enough for two people to recline on for a banquet and were made comfortable with long, mattress-like cushions. From the 8th century BC, the Greek furniture makers were using very slim legs for couches, some of which were turned, a form of support that is found on Egyptian and Persian furniture of the period.

Roman day-beds were even more closely related to Greek antecedents. Since couches were the most expensive items of furniture in the homes of well-to-do citizens, they were richly ornamented with bronze, ivory and bone. The sophistication of Roman furniture is seen in a sarcophagus of the 2nd century AD, which depicts a woman lying on a couch that has turned legs, a long padded seat and a high back – a good design that was in fact imitated in the 1830s. Couches with both long and short legs were used by the Romans, although at meals it was usually only the head of the household who reclined: the rest of the family sat on stools and chairs.

By the end of the 1st century AD, the characteristic Roman style, with a high back and sides – the forerunner of the popular modern sofa – had emerged. The Roman love of colour and comfort was seen in the sofa's geneously padded cushions and the brightly patterned mattress covers.

The construction of the more elegant Greek and Roman couches, which stood on delicate legs, was dependent on trained and disciplined craftsmen who carried their techniques across Europe. Some of these skills were never completely lost in the so-called Dark Ages, and excavations continually reveal instances of work of a higher quality than was once considered possible. Because of the unsettled lifestyle of the nobility in the early medieval period, and the constant moves from one castle to another, portable furniture became highly important. The basic construction of couches was very simple, but the piece was given importance by the use of costly drapery and cushions. By fixing some form of wall-hanging above a bench, this basic structure was transformed into a seat of honour. Because people lived and slept in the same room, beds often doubled as couches.

Court life in the late medieval period was lavish and colourful, with furniture and walls hung with tapestry and embroidery. By the mid-15th century, couches were found in rooms that also had a bed and they were obviously intended for daytime use. One low-backed French example had collapsible sides and was made more comfortable by the addition of tasselled cushions. Others had pierced-work sides in ecclesiastical designs reminiscent of the work of the great Gothic stone carvers. The typical Italian form of seat, the *cassapanca*, is also associated with the 15th century, and was a development of the traditional chest, known as a *cassone*. The *cassapanca* was provided with a low back and a seat that could be lifted. It was either painted or elaborately carved.

The couch had become the seat of honour in important houses by the beginning of the 17th century. Sometimes canopied, it would stand against a tapestry – or needlework-hung wall, and so did not need a back. The arms on the finest examples were adjustable and could be lowered by either a ratchet system or a series of rods. The 'Great Couches' of this type were either painted or covered with padded leather or fabric. The most famous example, popularly known as the 'Knole' sofa, dates to the second quarter of the century and is a later development, as its original high back shows that the piece was intended as a freestanding item.

Settees of the chair-back type were a development of the earlier court fashion of standing a row of chairs against one another on either side of a seat of honour or a state bed. Both carved and upholstered versions are characteristic of the second half of the 17th century, the most superb examples still retaining their original needlework or Genoa-velvet upholstery. The finest work of the period was created by French craftsmen, who fashioned prestige pieces for the court with gilded carving, sumptuous cushions, tassels and fringes.

The upholsterer's craft is seen at its best in the finest sofas of the late 17th century. Intended only for the very wealthy, they boasted opulent cut velvets, brocaded silks, fringes and tassels exported from France and Italy, thus allowing one piece of furniture to exhibit the products of several countries. After the revocation of the Edict of Nantes in 1685, French weavers and cabinet-makers, fleeing religious persecution, took their skills to other countries.

By the end of the 17th century, French furniture makers had begun to produce almost every type of basic sofa. The most characteristically French design was the *lit-de-repos*, with ornate gilded carving. Some versions had only one arm, which acted as a back rest and was obviously intended for reclining, while others had two sides so they could seat several people.

PRE-1700

1. An Ancient Egyptian Painting, featuring a Sofa with Animal Feet, *c*1000 BC

Ladies Listening to a Harpist are the subject of this Egyptian tempera painting of c1000 BC. It comes from the Valley of the Nobles, Thebes, and dates to the XXth Dynasty. From the Tomb of Inkerkha, it shows the deceased listening to a harpist and seated on a small, straight-backed sofa. The strutted framework beneath the seat was a popular construction method and acted as a brace as well as a decorative device. The animal-leg feet in this instance are quite simple, but in some seat furniture massive and well-carved lion-paw feet were used. Cheap woods were often gilded or painted to create a more lavish effect.

2. Modern Painting of Cleopatra by John Collier, featuring Early Egyptian Sofa with Animal Feet, *c*50 BC

In his interpretation of *The Death of Cleopatra*, John Collier (1850–1934) shows the Queen of the Nile reclining on the type of couch that could have been used in the period. Early Egyptian sofas were very simple, but by the 1st Dynasty legs with bull's feet were used. Lion-paw feet, in combination with lion masks at the head, appeared in the Middle Kingdom on the beds or settles of people of high rank. In the main, native woods such as tamarisk or acacia were used, although cedar and juniper were also imported. Sheet gold and gold leaf on gesso were employed (in this instance, gold enhances the headrest section). By the time of Cleopatra, couches were used for both daytime reclining as well as nocturnal sleeping. These ancient forms appear to have persisted and influenced much Roman furniture.

3. An Ancient Roman Wall Painting, featuring a 'Love Seat' *c*50 BC

In *Noblewoman Playing a Cithara*, a fresco dating to *c*50 BC, a woman sits on a small sofa, similar in size to love seats of the 18th century. The seat is supported on turned legs, strengthened with a brace, and its slatted back is curved for greater comfort. This piece reveals the complexity of form that was possible at the time. These early furniture-making methods were carried across Europe by the Romans but were lost during the Dark Ages, after which the development of modern European construction methods began.

2

PRE-1700

3

1

4. A Flemish Miniature Painting, featuring a Renaissance Upholstered Sofa, *c*1480

Comfort was not entirely absent from the homes of the wealthy in the 15th century. In this miniature from a manuscript of the *Chronique d'Angleterre*, by Jean de Wavrin, executed at Bruges for Edward IV in the late 1400s, John of Portugal is seen entertaining John of Gaunt. They sit on an upholstered sofa, covered in green fabric, with a high back and sides. The filling, probably sheep's wool or animal hair, was held in place by tufts. The green fabric was further decorated with a wave-like gold pattern. This is one of the simplest methods of constructing a padded sofa and has been repeated throughout the centuries. In the 15th century, only the most important people would have owned any upholstered furniture, ordinary folk using simple wooden settles akin to the bench seen in the painting's foreground.

5. A Flemish Painting by Pieter Bruegel the Elder, featuring Wooden Benches, *c*1568

In the *Peasant Wedding, c*1568, by Pieter Bruegel the Elder (*c*1525–69), most of the guests sit on simple benches. These have plank tops and legs made from roughly cut lengths of woods from which, in some cases, the bark has not been removed. Near the door is what appears to be a high-backed settle of more finished construction upon which the more important people sit. It has a plank back finished with a thicker top rail. The side supports are made of square-cut sections of wood. It is obvious that this piece of furniture is the most significant item in this Flemish peasant interior.

6. An English William & Mary Upholstered Sofa, *c*1690

Dating to *c*1690, this sofa of the William & Mary period is of that style's typical form, wherein each seat area is reflected both by legs and supporting stretchers. The simple square shape is embellished with bobbin-turning to the legs and stretchers, while the upholstery of the back, seat and arms is finished with a deep fringe, the standard decorative practice at the time. Such pieces could only have been afforded by the relatively wealthy, and consequently few have survived; those that do appear on the market now command high prices.

5

4

6

PRE-1700

7. An English Gilt-Wood Day-Bed, c1695

This day-bed, from Temple Newsam House in Leeds, was made c1695 for the Duke of Leeds. A sofa at its most princely, it is part of a suite, also incuding a high-backed sofa with arms (see Ill. 8), which was made for the Duke's manor, Kiveton Park, in Yorkshire. Both this day-bed and the sofa have stretchers in the same form and are upholstered in Genoa silk velvet in reds and greens on a typical cream background. It was an interest in comfort that fostered the construction of such day-beds; this gilt-wood example, with its tasselled fringe, is especially fine, in that attention was given to the carving of its frame as well as to its upholstery.

8. An English Gilt-Wood Settee, c1695

This fabulous settee from Temple Newsam House is one of the great classics in the history of British furniture. Made c1695, it is over 7 ft (2.1 m) long and made in the princely manner. Matching the day-bed (Ill. 7) and, like that piece, very much in the French taste, the straight back is crested by three escutcheons bearing the cipher and coronet of the 1st Duke of Leeds (Thomas Osborne, created duke in 1694). It is upholstered in Genoa velvet, one of the most fashionable coverings of the period, and is elaborately fringed and tasselled. Although the upholstery is original, it was rearranged in the 20th century, perhaps to conceal areas of heavy wear. The extravagant use of fringe and braids is typical of the period, although the cost was so high that furniture in this manner would only have been owned by the very wealthy. The day-bed and settee were originally made for Kiveton Park in Yorkshire, home of the 1st Duke of Leeds, but both are now at Temple Newsam House in Leeds.

9. An Indian Watercolour, featuring a Sofa-Type Throne, c1700

In this watercolour, painted c1700 by an anonymous Rajasthan artist, Rama is shown with Ramasita, Oakshman and Hamuman. They are seated on a high-backed, sofa-type throne which stands on four legs. Such polygonal thrones were a traditional Indian form, and the top section of some could be lifted off by decorative handles. In this version the cushion is richly embroidered and the wood appears to be inlaid with coloured stones. Upholstered Indian thrones of the same period with shaped arms are also recorded.

9

8

7

1700
TO
1800

The 18th century witnessed the transition from generally crude furniture constructions concealed by rich upholstery, to pieces of a degree of sophistication and superb craftsmanship that have never been surpassed. Although the period is dominated by the names of the great arbiters of fashion such as Adam, Chippendale and Sheraton, there were hundreds of small businesses producing unexciting seat furniture for local customers. Other provincial carpenters and joiners imitated the more adventurous designs shown in pattern-books, which were readily available because of improvements in printing. The publication of these books, with their crisp line drawings of progressive designs and suggestions for suitable woods and fabrics, meant that sophisticated 'city styles' could be reproduced by any good craftsman, hence resulting in some superb regional work.

As travel between countries became easier, French and Italian designs exerted a greater influence on British and American furniture, although the styles were often adapted with so much restraint that their confident originality was lost. After 1750, French taste became all-important, especially in the design of sofas, whose high arms became a virtual continuation of the back. In some Adam versions, the serpentine backs sweep forward in a bold, unbroken line, while the covering fabric is spread generously in a pleasing, rounded shape – ideal for showing off the fine brocaded silks of the period.

In the early 18th century, the most progressive seat furniture was made for great houses and palaces but, by the 1760s, cabinet-makers' design books were also suggesting up-to-date pieces for the homes of gentlefolk of moderate means. While a heavily ornamented sofa might be suggested for a wealthy patron, there were also many simpler versions that could be selected by a small-town lawyer or doctor. This gradual shift in emphasis, from the taste of the nobility to the needs of a growing middle class, resulted in a great increase in the number of manufacturers, many of whom are known through the labels and marks they applied to sofa frames. French furniture enthusiasts are especially fortunate, since, after 1751, every item was required to be stamped with the maker's name, a system that, unfortunately, was not enforced in Great Britain or America.

Some of the most splendid 18th-century sofas were designed as components of large suites of furniture. Intent on creating interiors of perfection, architects such as William Kent found it necessary to develop furniture styles that were completely in accord with the structure of a room; thus, tables, stools and massive pairs of sofas were all conceived as part of a grand composition. Kent, with his extravagant interpretation of Italian styles, dominated fashionable taste in the early years of the century; his sculptural sofas, ornamented with shells, animal heads, sphinxes, cherubs and leaves, sometimes resembled stone monuments rather than functional furnishings. When these carved sofas were gilded or painted, they were usually made of relatively cheap pine.

As mahogany became more widely used, due to the increasing scarcity of walnut, the styles of seat furniture became much lighter. No longer was upholstery fabric seen as the most important element of a sofa as in the 17th century. Instead the show-wood came to dominate a piece; and makers competed to produce the most delicate creations. By the 1750s, sofas were an accepted part of the furnishing of any gentleman's house and there were various styles for the hall, drawing room, boudoir or library. The simplest were given drop-in seats and wooden backs, a type that remained popular for use in entrance halls until the 20th century, when many reproductions of early styles were reintroduced. The chairback type of sofa, first seen in the 17th century, was very popular. Some of the most interesting were upholstered in needlework depicting biblical or classical scenes, which give the furniture a handsome period effect. Most of this needlework was produced commercially, but occasionally sets of gros- or petit-point covers were worked by the ladies of the house.

Thomas Chippendale designed some of the most elegant sofas of the chair-back type, perhaps the most characteristic being in the ribbon-back form, a delicate style that was especially suited to mahogany. More in sympathy with general European taste were the upholstered sofas Chippendale illustrated in *The Gentleman and Cabinet-Maker's Director*, first published in 1754; these designs revealed the increasing importance of comfort. In general, Chippendale furniture was made on a scale more suitable for houses than castles and his sofas varied from 6 to 10 ft (1.8 to 3 m) long. For additional comfort, he suggested a matching bolster at each end, as well as square back cushions. The elegance and lightness of the structures were emphasized by the show-wood, which was used more as a decorative border than an integral part of the structure. Despite this interest in the general market, Chippendale sofas in the grand manner – with lavish gilded carving, whose cherubs and classical figures could be relied upon to create an atmosphere of opulence – were still deemed necessary for splendid rooms.

Chippendale's 'couches', in fact comfortable armchairs with the seats extended and supported on six or eight legs, are among the most elegant of sofa designs. This French sofa form was ideal for bedrooms as well as somewhat feminine drawing rooms; also, it was readily adaptable, since the cost depended on the quality of the upholstery and trimmings. Chippendale disliked many of the current designs that were intended to be taken apart to form an armchair and a stool and recommended that his own couches be single units of furniture. His 'Chinese style' sofa, a playful mixture of Rococo chinoiserie, is very much in the grand 17th-century idiom, and was placed against drapery with a canopy for added importance. This sofa could be converted into a bed by letting down the arms, a versatility that was not uncommon in 18th-century designs.

In 18th-century Europe, French furniture styles were all-important. Elegant sofas made in the Rue de Cléry area of Paris were exported to Germany and Russia for the homes of the most discerning. These sofas were made of oak, beech or walnut and were polished, painted or gilded. Among the large variety of sofa styles made was the curved *confident*, or *tête-à-tête*, on which two or three people sat facing in opposite directions, thus enabling them to whisper discreetly. Such pieces often formed a part of the large suites of salon furniture, which could also include several sofas and *lits-de-repos*, all upholstered in Gobelins tapestry or ravishingly coloured Lyons silk brocade.

The period of revolution in Europe swept away the last vestiges of frivolous Rococo and heralded a new Classicism, which favoured simpler antique forms once used by the Egyptians and the Greeks. Embroidered and brocaded covers were discarded and sofas were finished in restrained fabrics more suited to the new democratic lifestyle. This Classicism was seen at its most refined in northern Europe, but British and American designers seem to have appreciated the cleaner, more academic lines that revealed the quality of workmanship rather than obscuring it with ornament.

10. A French Régence Gilt-Wood Canapé, 1700–35

From a suite of Régence furniture, this fine canapé was made in France in the 18th century. The cresting of the back rail is especially decorative, and there is an equally ornate apron to the seat front. The term 'Régence' is often used rather loosely to cover the period from 1700 to 1735, The suite also included four *fauteuils* (upholstered chairs with open arms). Upholstered in leather and standing on six cabriole legs, this Rococo piece's construction is derived from chair-back forms. Rarely does furniture of this quality appear on the international market.

11. An English Queen Anne Walnut Love Seat, *c*1710

A small early 18th-century walnut sofa, this piece is reupholstered in saffron silk. This version, with a rectangular back, has well-shaped low scrolled arms and stands on cabriole legs with hoof feet, enriched with restrained carving on the knee. Known as a 'love seat' because of its small size, such sofas were sometimes constructed in the chair-back style, with pierced central splats which must have made them very uncomfortable. Others have needlework upholstery, sometimes in combination with gilt-wood, giving them a regal effect. Less romantically, it seems probable that these sofa/chairs were made to accommodate the voluminous skirts of ladies of fashion more comfortably.

12. An English George I Mahogany Love Seat with Needlework Upholstery, *c*1720

Small-sized sofas such as this one were popularly known as 'love seats' and were ideal pieces for the display of needlework. This particularly attractive George I example, with gros- and petit-point needlework, was made c1720. The mahogany sofa has a shaped back and high scrolled arms with curvilinear supports. It stands on cabriole legs with carved volutes. Such sofas were mainly used in reception rooms and could be placed near a tea or card table.

10

12

11

13. A French Régence Beechwood Sofa with Needlework Upholstery, *c1720*

Early 18th-century French furniture was lighter and more sophisticated than its British counterpart. This sofa, carved in beechwood, was made in the Régence period (1715–23) of Louis XV's reign. The delicacy of its scrolled legs, joined by waved cross-stretchers carved with flowers, is typical of the best work made within the guild system, which encouraged the development of the various crafts involved in the construction of seat furniture. The sofa's value, however, depends not so much on the carcase as on the quality of the superb needlework upholstery, which depicts Venus attended by nymphs and putti, together with animals, shells, leaves and flowers. The rich design is executed in gros- and petit-point needlework in wool and silk on a dark brown background. The panel on the serpentine seat shows a lion chasing a stag.

13

14. A Dutch Painted Hall Bench, *c*1720

Furniture that is especially made for hall seating is, almost invariably, highly decorative but extremely uncomfortable. This green-painted hall bench dates from the early 18th century and was part of the furnishings of a Dutch home. The houses of the Dutch merchant classes in the 1700s were much more lavishly equipped than those of their German or English counterparts, and in the main reception furniture was intended to impress. This hall bench has an ornately carved large central shell centred among attractive pierced work. The shallow carving of the decorative apron is a typical Dutch feature of the period.

15. An English George I Walnut Settle, *c*1725

The height of the back of this double chair-back walnut settle is relatively low, a good feature that suggests a date of around 1725. The flat uprights are given more interest by the carved decoration at the top, and the line of the back uprights mirrors the shape of the back splats, thus giving the piece a pleasing unity. The cabriole legs have the typical shell-carved knees and the ball-and-claw feet that were so popular with British makers, and the gentle shaping of the back made the chair quite comfortable as well. A weak feature, however, is the shallow seat rail, which lacks ornamentation.

16. A French Louis XV Gilt-Wood Canapé, *c*1725–30

This fine early Louis XV gilt-wood canapé dates to the second quarter of the 18th century. The term 'canapé' refers to high-backed French sofas in Louis XV style, although it is also used more loosely to describe any French-style sofa with closed sides. The serpentine top rail is carved with flowerheads and scrolling acanthus leaves, flanked by shells and wave motifs. The down-swept armrests are carved with foliage and shells and incised with latticework. The carving to the serpentine front of the seat complements the back rest, which is also decorated on the reverse with shells and foliage. The cabriole legs end in foliate carved scrolled toes. The canapé was once in the collection of the Art Institute of Chicago.

16

17. A French Louis XV Walnut Canapé

The close nailing of the upholstery makes a positive contribution to the design of this small French canapé. Made of walnut, the canapé stands on six moulded cabriole legs with scroll feet. The shaping of the seat front is reminiscent of the chair form, although the back is made in one piece. The moulded outset arms feature scrolls and padded elbow rests. The sofa is upholstered in rose damask, with a needlework fruiting-vine border with ornamental corners continuing on the squab cushion. The originality of the upholstery makes this canapé especially appealing.

18. A French Louis XV Walnut Canapé with Tapestry Upholstery

A delicate and small canapé, this piece was made in France in the 18th century. The undulating double curve of the back rail is repeated, unusually, on the lower edge of the back rest. Made of walnut, the canapé stands on delicate cabriole legs. The double serpentine fronts of the seat rail are centred with carved motifs. The tapestry upholstery is in good condition and depicts figures in a colourful landscape.

19. An English George II Gold- and White-Painted Beechwood Sofa, c1735

Painted in white and gold, this dramatic beechwood sofa was made c1735. A sofa such as this would have been an integral part of a complete decorative scheme, commissioned by a very wealthy patron. All the woodwork was covered and rich fabrics used for the upholstery, so that the magnificent effect of an Italian palace could be re-created. The use of carved swags, shells, mythological beasts, fruit and leaves set against abundant scrolls was all typical of the designs of William Kent (c1686–1748) and his followers. Kent's influence extended into all spheres of educated taste, even though it was retrospective in idiom and demanded a degree of craftsmanship that was extremely expensive. Complete suites of furniture in the heavy Baroque taste that marks this sofa filled the homes of many wealthy British noblemen.

18

19

20. An English George II Mahogany Sofa, *c*1740

This heavily carved English mahogany sofa was made around 1740. Impressive pieces of this kind were often constructed as one of a pair and would originally have been upholstered in silk or velvet. Shaped high backs of this type are usually completely upholstered, the carved arm supports thereby adding interest. Originally one long squab cushion would have been fitted rather than the three replacements. The carved cabriole legs are finished with heavily ornamented volutes. Though somewhat florid in construction, the piece would sell well as it is so typical of the period.

21. An English George II Mahogany Sofa, *c*1740

From around 1740, the arms of sofas and chairs became much higher and, as in this example, are often a virtual continuation of the back. This English George II mahogany sofa has nicely shaped cabriole legs, terminating in ball-and-claw feet. The shallow seat rail is decorated with central carved motifs. It has six legs to give added support because of length; hence it clearly shows how the sofa form developed from the chair-back types. The seat-rail pendants give added interest, although obviously the piece would be much more valuable if it had the original, or a later tapestry or needlework, covering. In the mid-18th century, both damask and leather were used, as well as velvet.

22. An English George II Double Chair-Back Walnut Sofa, *c*1740

Made in England *c*1740, this George II walnut double chair-back sofa has a somewhat clumsy form. Originally the seat would have been upholstered in needlework or velvet: the unattractive striped upholstery is especially unfortunate. The out-scrolled arms are raised on acanthus-carved supports, whereas the well-shaped cabriole legs are carved at the knees with a mantled cabochon flanked by acanthus leaves; they terminate in paw feet. The chair backs have pierced-work splats decorated with flowerheads and acanthus leaves. As flat splats are much more common, an example with this amount of ornamentation always commands interest, especially, as in this case, when the sofa is one of a pair.

23. An Italian Walnut Sofa from the Palazzo Rezzonico, Venice, *c*1745–50

Sofas of this type were made for use in Italian ballrooms or the very long rooms that extended the depth of a Venetian palace. This most elegant example dates to the mid-18th century and was made for the Palazzo Rezzonico in Venice. The undulating, carved back rail is centred with a shell and supported on a pierced splat. The carved apron of the seat rail contributes to the overall delicate effect. This sofa is part of a matching set of furniture, which also includes a larger version with three back splats and standing on ten cabriole legs. Large sofas of this type were ideal for use in a ballroom as they could be moved easily to allow for dancing.

24. An Italian Triple Chair-Back Gilt-Wood Sofa, *c*1745–50

A triple chair-back gilded sofa made in Venice in the mid-18th century for the Palazzo Rezzonico. The chair backs are centred with carved foliate crests, devices that are repeated on the seat rail. By the mid-18th century, French influence on Italian furniture was very strong and the Italian nobility began to use smaller items of furniture for the more intimate types of rooms which were becoming more fashionable. For many years the heavy, palatial styles associated with the 17th century remained popular in Italy, but gradually lighter furniture began to be made by native craftsmen who had often been trained in France. In thier imitative work they often exaggerated the decorative forms to create pieces that were sufficiently impressive for the Venetian palaces.

24

23

22

1700-1800

25. An English George II Sofa with Needlework Upholstery, *c*1750

A nicely proportioned English-made sofa of *c*1750, its shaped back and high, scrolled arms characterize the period. It stands on simple square legs united by plain stretchers. Sofas of this type were ideal for the display of needlework, which was often worked by the women of the household – although a large number were also commercially produced. After 1775, needlework covered sofas were replaced with silk or tapestry upholstery. In the 19th century it again became fashionable to work sets of covers for antique furniture, a practice that has continued to the present day.

26. An English George II Ebonized-Wood Sofa, *c*1750

From a suite of George II furniture, this sofa with a plain rectangular back has an ebonized finish. The cabriole legs are carved with acanthus leaves. Close nailing is used to accentuate the square form of the seat padding.

27. An English George II Gilt-Wood Sofa, *c*1750

This mid-18th-century gilt-wood sofa was later reupholstered in velvet. Massive, heavily carved sofas were usually part of a large saloon suite, all parts of which would be covered in matching fabric. The architectural style of the piece is reminiscent of William Kent's work. A very ornate back crest was a feature of many sofas of the George II period, as this impressive detail gave the piece added importance. This was still furniture in the grand manner, intended for mansions and castles. As the carved wood was covered with gesso and gilding, cheaper materials – especially pine – were used for the construction.

28. An English George II Gilt-Wood Sofa, *c*1750

The very pleasant curve of this sofa's serpentine back, in combination with its fairly deep seat rail, contributes to a highly pleasing piece of mid-18th-century English furniture. Made during the reign of George II, the gilt-wood sofa has out-scrolled arms centring a rectangular seat. The seat rail is carved with Vitruvian scrolls terminating in square motifs. The well shaped cabriole legs are carved with pendent bellflowers that are flanked by scrolls; the feet are also scrolled. The later upholstery does not detract from the value of such a fine example from an especially favoured period.

26

27

25

28

29. An English George II Double Chair-Back Mahogany Sofa in Chippendale Style, c1750–60

This superb carved-mahogany, double chair-back sofa of the mid-18th century is similar in form to examples designed by Thomas Chippendale (1718–79). The ribbon-back of this sofa, so called because the carving was made to resemble crimped ribbon, makes the piece highly desirable. Chippendale made several sets of what he termed 'Ribband-Back' chairs, all of which had given 'entire satisfaction'. In his *Gentleman and Cabinetmaker's Director*, he suggested that the seats could be covered with red Morocco leather for an especially fine effect. This sofa incorporates sections from several of the chair designs in the *Director*. The Victoria and Albert Museum, owner of this example, considers it to be the work of Chippendale himself, who was a master woodcarver. In the highly ornamental Rococo designs of this type, Chippendale was following the French styles first seen at the court of Louis XV. Such exquisite 18th-century work is unsurpassed.

29

30

28

30. An English Georgian Oak Settle, *c*1750–60

Oak settles of this type were originally intended mainly for use in large halls, but are now popular for dining rooms. In this simple 18th-century design, the back has four plain panels. The shaped legs that are continued into the turned arm supports are of unusual form, as is the centre leg that seems almost an afterthought to provide additional support. The squab cushion rests on wooden slats, although in some versions cord was strung across the seat. There are many variations on this basic form, as country makers in each area made these very practical pieces in some number. Throughout the 19th and early 20th centuries similar pieces were made, especially for use in hotels and pubs.

31. An English George II Sofa, designed by Thomas Chippendale, *c*1759

This is one of Chippendale's most elegant designs for a sofa, published in 1759. He recommended that the structures be made from 6 ft to 9 or 10 ft long (1.8m to 2.7–3m long). The depth of the seat from front to back, he suggested, should be 2 ft 3 in to 3 ft (.7m to 1m), and the height of the seat (including the castors) 1 ft 2 in (.4m). He felt that the seats should be deep enough for the sofa to be used as an occasional bed. In his design book, Chippendale claimed that all the drawings could be executed by a skilful workman, although at the time many complained that some of the more extreme creations, especially those in the Chinese manner, were almost impossible to copy. This type of sofa was of a plainer form, however, and has been constructed, with adaptations, by generations of cabinetmakers.

31

32. An English George II Sofa, designed by Thomas Chippendale, c1759

The larger versions of this 1759 Chippendale sofa design were provided with a bolster and pillow at each end and cushions at the back 'that may be laid down occasionally to form a mattress'. The 'circular' back corners of this design were obviously considered very progressive by the designer and exhibit the influence of French taste. An inset drawing suggested that this seat could be made in the Gothic style by using rectangular-type legs decorated with quasi-ecclesiastical carving. The line drawings naturally make the sofas seem very light and delicate: when constructed, they have a much heavier effect, as the wood probably could not be worked so delicately by other cabinetmakers. Chippendale claimed that in his workshops every design could be improved 'both as to beauty and enrichment'.

33. A French Louis XV Gilt-Wood Day-Bed by Jean-Baptiste Tilliard, second half of 18th century

An ornate and typically French 18th-century day-bed of carved and gilded wood, this example bears the stamp of Jean-Baptiste Tilliard (1685–1766). Its apron's decoration echoes that of its back, and a drop-in squab cushion provided the comfort that furniture buyers were demanding at the time. Cushions of this type were usually filled with curled horsehair. In 1743, French master craftsmen were obliged to stamp their work, an aspect of the strict guild system that has made it possible to trace the development of style, even within individual families. Tilliard *père* and *fils* were among the leading *menuisiers* who passed the craft from father to son.

32

35

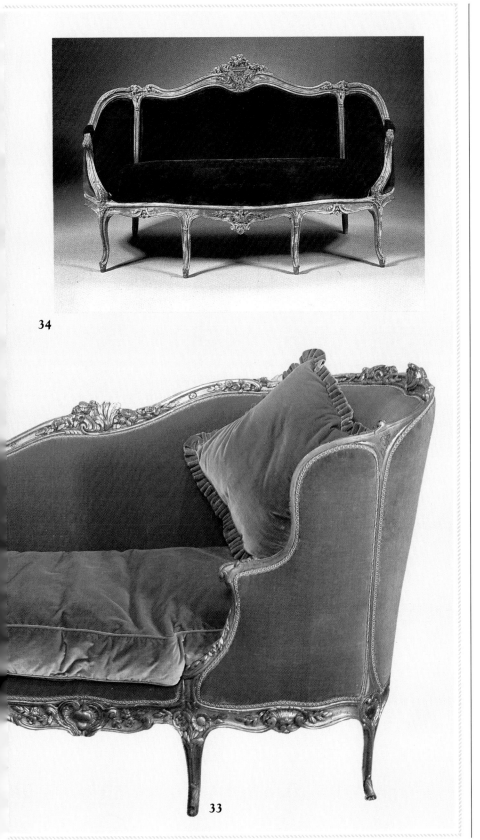

34

33

34. A French Louis XVI Beechwood Canapé en Corbeille, c1750–75

Made in the manner of Nicolas-Quinibert Foliot (1706–76), this fine beechwood canapé en Corbeille dates to the third quarter of the 18th century. Its complex serpentine back is centred with a flower-filled urn flanked by acanthus leaves. The arms have voluted supports carved with trailing, budding veins. The padded, upholstered seat has a conforming seat rail carved with ribbon-tied floral bouquets and the apron is carved with laurel and scrolling foliage. The cabriole legs end in foliate scroll toes. Similar sofas are known with the stamp of 'N. Q. Foliot'. The Foliot family were members of the guild of the *menuisiers* who passed their skills from father to son and worked according to strict rules delineating the functions of the various furniture craftsmen.

35. An English George III Triple Chair-Back Walnut Settle

Chair-back settles evolved from the practice of placing a row of chairs close together, against walls or on either side of a state bed or a seat of honour. Despite the fact that they were often not very comfortable – as in this model, intended for three people to sit together – the form continued to be popular until the 1900s. This triple chair-back settle, in attractively figured walnut, is not as well proportioned as the best early 18th-century examples and the shaping of the top of the central leg is weak. Also, the carving of the top of the shell on the uprights is too fussy, as is that of the joining shells between the chair backs.

36. A Continental Parcel-Gilt Triple Chair-Back Settee in Rococo Style, *c1760*

Each section of this triple chair-back settle, made *c1760*, is centred with a carved crest, and the knees are robustly carved. Although highly decorative, the parcel-gilt structure lacks the elegance of some of the best English work; rather, it reflects the more ostentatious Continental Rococo taste which was practiced in Italy and imitated in Germany.

37. An English Georgian Hump-back Settee in Chippendale Style, *c1760*

Typically Chippendale in style is this mahogany 'hump-back' settee with scrolling spandrels. Made in England *c1760*, the settee's seat rail is decorated with the blind fret that characterizes so many Chippendale designs. The sofa designs illustrated in the master's *Director* reveal his most complex and expensive work, but simpler constructions such as this were also made in some number for sale through his shop in St Martin's Lane, London, and to the many customers for whom he furnished entire houses. Chippendale trained a large number of craftsmen who imitated his designs when they set up their own businesses, some in America, where furniture in the classical Chippendale style was also produced. The Chippendale furniture style, whose effect depends on fine materials and good craftsmanship, has never gone out of style.

38. An English George III Sofa in Chippendale Style, *c1760*

Dating to the reign of George III, this mahogany sofa is constructed in Chippendale style. In his *Director*, Chippendale illustrated a chair with similarly shaped arms and an upholstered back with small side projections; such chairs were described as 'French chairs'. This double chair-back sofa stands on square legs linked by plain stretchers. The brackets joining the legs and seat are a feature of pieces in Chippendale style.

38

36

37

39. An English George III Mahogany Sofa, 1760s

This Georgian sofa presents a striking appearance because of its exaggerated scroll-arms. Made of mahogany, it dates to the 1760s. The square chamfered and stop-fluted legs are joined by plain stretchers. Mahogany only came into general use in the British furniture trade after 1750, when Cuban as well as Jamaican imports became available. Honduras mahogany was also used extensively in the late 18th century. Mahogany was an ideal wood for sofas, as it remained strong even when heavily carved or when thinly cut to form slender legs or delicate stretchers. As the qualities of the wood became more appreciated, stretchers were no longer a necessity and were included more for their decorative qualities than to give added strength to a piece.

40. An English George III Mahogany Corner Sofa, 1760s

This George III mahogany sofa was especially made for use in a corner position. Dating to the late 1760s, the piece is unusual because of its shape. The settee is also of good general quality and has a shaped padded back, terminating on either side with scroll elbow supports, and a moulded mahogany frame, standing on square front supports. The castors are later, as is the coiled springing of the seat. When reupholstered in the 18th-century style, this sofa would present a much finer appearance, especially when the unsightly rectangular, fringed cushion is eliminated.

41. An English George III Sofa Design by Robert Adam, 1762

Robert Adam (1738–92) designed this delicate sofa in 1762 for Lord Scarsdale. The classical details on the arms and back rail are typical of Adam's interpretation of the styles of Greece and Rome. Simple neo-Classical furniture of this type brought a refreshing lightness into English drawing rooms and Adam's designs were soon widely imitated. Adam's sofa designs were intended for pieces about 12 ft (3.6 m) long that were to be gilded. This specific example was also executed for a 'Mrs Montagu in Hill Street'. London furniture maker John Linnell (c1737–96) was responsible for the construction of many sofas to Adam's drawings, but his interpretation was often quite exuberant and used as a vehicle to display his carving skills.

42. An English George III Mahogany Sofa, c1765

An English-made mahogany sofa, this dates to around 1765, to the reign of George III. The serpentine cresting rail of the back continues, in a well-defined curve, to the sharply downward-sloping arms, which are padded. The attractive gadrooned border is repeated on the front of the serpentine seat. The cabriole legs are headed by mantled cabochons and end in delicate scrolled feet. As this Georgian piece is only 5 ft (1.5 m) long, its size makes it especially desirable. Its somewhat restrained interpretation of the exuberant French Rococo style is more in accordance with British and American taste.

43. An English George III Mahogany Sofa, 1770s

From a suite of furniture, this George III mahogany sofa stands on long cabriole legs with carving and scrolled feet, lending it slightly ungainly proportions. Such high sofas were used as seating around card tables or for eating supper, and sometimes appear unsatisfactory or awkward when seen in isolation. The curved padding of the front is more typical of the work of French upholsterers.

42

39

41

43

40

1700-1800

44. A French Louis XVI Gilt-Wood Canapé by Georges Jacob, *c*1775

This canapé is part of a suite of Louis XVI gilt-wood furniture also comprising four armchairs. Although made as one of a set, the sofa's rectangular back is in complete contrast to the rounded chair backs. The frame of the canapé is carved with leaf tips and continuous laurel banding, and its conforming seat rail is sculpted with leaf tips and berried laurel. It stands on circular, stop-fluted legs that taper and are headed by paterae and gadrooned capitals; they end in *toupie* (or 'top') feet. The suite is stamped 'G. Jacob', the mark of Georges Jacob (1739–1814), an innovative maker of carved seat furniture who introduced more formal, rectangular elements into his work in the last quarter of the 18th century.

45

Mahogany Settee with Needlework Upholstery, *c*1775

A very elegant George III settee with an attractive serpentine curved back rest, this piece dates to around 1775. It has beautifully scrolled arms of slim form that contribute to its elegant structure, and the square-shaped legs are carved with mantled cabochons. With mahogany show-wood, the sofa is especially desirable because of the needlepoint upholstery, worked in gros- and petit-point and depicting various exotic animals, including an elephant. The shaping of the centre of the front rail is an unusual feature. It is probable that the squab cushion was also originally covered with matching embroidery.

46. An Italian Neo-Classical Gilt-Wood Settee, *c*1775–1800

With its superb craftsmanship, Italian and French furniture design dominated Europe in the 18th century. This gilt-wood settee dates to the third quarter of the 18th century and was possibly made in Piedmont. Many Piedmontese craftsmen had originally worked in France, so they often adapted French designs in a more ornate, typically Italianate manner. This neo-Classical example has a curved back that continues in a firm curve to form the arms. A portrait medallion, framed with ribbon-tied twin cornucopias, centres the back. The arms end in rams' heads above acanthus-carved supports. The seat rail is carved with leaves above trailing scrolled foliage and husks that centre yet another portrait medallion. The spiral-fluted cabriole legs are sculpted with acanthus leaves and terminate in acanthus-carved scrolled toes.

44

46

45

1700-1800

47. A French Louis XVI Gilt-Wood Canapé, attributed to Georges Jacob, c1775–1800

A very formal French gilt-wood canapé, this example dates to the last quarter of the 18th century. Made in a gentle interpretation of the Renaissance manner, it features a rectangular back, which was more popular in Germany and other northern European countries than in France. The sofa is attributed to Georges Jacob (1739–1814) who was one of the leading *menuisiers* of the time. He originally worked in a typical Louis XV style, but gradually introduced neo-Classical features into his work. In the last 25 years of the century, when this canapé was made, Jacob was continually adding new elements to his seat furniture. The curves of the Louis XV style were steadily abandoned and, by 1800, straight, more formal lines were preferred. The frame of this sofa is carved with festoons of fruit and flowers and the slightly out-scrolled armrests have laurel-decorated columnar supports. It stands on circular fluted legs that gently taper.

48. An English Cream-Painted and Parcel-Gilt Sofa in Hepplewhite Style, c1780

This Hepplewhite-style sofa was made c1780. By the last quarter of the 18th century, squab cushions were no longer very fashionable, although they continued to be used occasionally. In this version, the seat padding is fixed to the seat rail. In his *Guide* of 1788, Hepplewhite suggested that the woodwork of sofas should be 'either mahogany or japanned in accordance with the chairs'. As he considered the sofa to be part of a suite of furniture, he also advocated the use of matching coverings. This cream-painted and parcel-gilt version is in the more severe taste associated with the period. The back is almost rectangular but softens at the corners before it sweeps down to the straight sides, which are fitted with elbow rests. The sofa stands on turned and fluted legs, and its seat rail is carved with a central decoration.

49

50

48

47

49. An English George III Settle, c1780

Settles of this type were especially made throughout the 18th century for use in halls and garden rooms. As they were only intended for occasional seating, they were not provided with cushions or upholstery. This George III example is of a much higher quality than usual and is given additional interest by its arched central panel. The arms are well shaped and the carving of the seat rail also indicates a quality piece, one that no doubt originally occupied the hall of an important house. In the 19th century, the central panels of hall settles were sometimes overcarved with a family crest or even a royal cipher.

50. An English George III Mahogany Sofa, c1780

The simple and uncluttered line of this late 18th-century English sofa has a timeless quality. Such furniture does not move in and out of fashion but is considered classic, always favoured by the more conservative section of the antique trade and attractive to the investment buyer. Made around 1780, during the reign of George III, the sofa is of mahogany and is fitted with a squab cushion. Its serpentine back is padded and is continued to form the arms, which are fitted with elbow rests. It stands on square, fluted legs which taper and end in spade feet.

1700-1800

51. A French Louis XVI Walnut Canapé with Tapestry Upholstery, c1780s

The effect of much French seat furniture depended largely on the tapestry or needlework upholstery covering it. The Gobelins factory produced sets of tapestries that included panels for chairs and firescreens, as well as wall-hangings. Good quality French tapestry was made throughout the 19th century and was often employed to re-cover much earlier furniture for use in the drawing room or salon. The oval back of this walnut canapé is an ideal vehicle for the display of a romantic landscape. The light structure of this late 18th-century sofa and its rounded form were the marks of a French style that was to be copied and adapted in Britain; Robert Adam, in particular, favoured this type of structure.

52. A French Louis XVI Gilt-Wood Sofa, 1780s

In this Louis XVI gilt-wood sofa, the transition from the organic serpentine designs of the mid-18th century to the rectangular forms that characterized the late period can be seen. This two-seater sofa comes from a salon suite and is bordered with foliate carving. Padded armrests make a concession to comfort. Such sofas were intended for formal use, although they could also be used at card tables. Seating of this type, but in a much simplified form, was made for many middle-class homes in the early years of the 19th century.

53. An English George III Painted-Wood and Soft-Upholstered Sofa, 1780s

By the late 18th century, English sofas were made with a greater awareness of comfort. The square-sided cushions and the straight front to the seat of this George III sofa are elements of a particularly English upholstery method of the period. To create the 'square stuffed' effect, layers of padding were stitched above one another to give a crisp edge, which could then be accentuated with piping. Soft settees of this type were often criticized, as they were said to encourage indolence and lounging. The tapered legs of the 1780s sofa are painted.

53

51

52

54. An English George III Mahogany Settle, c1780–90

This late 18th-century mahogany high-backed settle features three fielded panels on its back. The balluster supports to the arms are in 17th-century style. Extra stability was given by the thin seat rails with their cross supports. Country pieces of this type are difficult to date precisely as designs in remote areas changed little until the mid-19th century and, as well, construction methods were somewhat static.

55. An English George III Carved and Painted Sofa, c1780–90

The formal elegance of this late 18th-century sofa would appeal to any buyer furnishing a home in George III style. The shaping of the serpentine back is pleasing, as is the line of the scrolled arms. The sofa is supported on carved and painted cabriole legs, which feature unusual Gothic-style tracery in combination with acanthus-leaf decoration on the feet. It is now reupholstered in damask and is fitted with the usual squab cushion.

56. An English George III Mahogany Sofa, c1785–95

This simple late 18th-century sofa stands on tapered legs of square form united by stretchers. It has a serpentine back and high padded arms. Plain but well-made furniture in mahogany was preferred for the furnishing of gentlemen's homes in Britain and the United States and this basic style has been adapted and reproduced throughout the centuries. Because of the honesty of their construction, pieces in this restrained George III manner were favoured when more ornate sofas were discarded.

57. An English George III Gilt-Wood Sofa, c1785–95

This George III gilded sofa comes from a late 18th-century drawing-room suite. The graceful curve of the serpentine back is broken by the upholstered armrests. Sofas with arms that are a continuation of the back were derived from French canapés. In Britain, Robert Adam popularized an even lighter form with turned, fluted legs. Silk damask was one of the favourite upholstery materials of the period, although the colours were much stronger than in this re-covered example, 'crimson India silk' or brilliant yellows being among the preferred hues.

57

54

56

55

1700-1800

58. An English George III Painted-Wood Sofa, c1785–1800

A late 18th-century sofa, this features a padded rectangular back and a wooden border with padded armrests. Painted in pale grey, the sofa stands on slim, reeded legs with spiral balusters extending to the fronts of the arms; the reeded legs are very typical of the period. The severity of the rectangular form of the back rest points towards the more geometric designs of the turn of the century. In the 1780s and 1790s, comfort was still an adjunct of wealth and luxury, and the seat was supplied with a mattress-like cushion – an expensive item, as upholstery frequently cost more than the wooden frame.

59. An English George III Gilt-Wood Sofa, c1790

Standing on eight cabriole legs, this George III gilt-wood sofa has a serpentine back. The knees and the front apron are decorated with shell and foliate carving. This sofa is in the manner of John Linnell (1729–96), a carver, cabinetmaker and designer, who worked out of London for many wealthy clients and also made furniture to Robert Adam's designs. Many of his original drawings have survived. So fine is some of Linnell's work that it is difficult to ascertain whether he or Robert Adam was responsible for certain pieces, notably at Osterley Park in Middlesex. This sofa is obviously one made 'in the grand manner', and was intended for a very wealthy customer.

60. A Continental Gilt-Wood Sofa showing Adam influence, c1790

The large rooms of Italian palaces and German castles in the late 18th century demanded a dramatic style of furniture. This gilt sofa, c1790, would have been sufficiently ostentatious to satisfy any ruler of a small German state. Standing on ten tapered and fluted legs, the heavily carved and gilt structure is in the sculptural style originally associated with Italy. The carved back rail is crested with a device incorporating a shield and a quiver of arrows, and the arm supports terminate in stylized heads. The putti were also a very popular form of decoration, especially on the Continent. Pine was often used for heavily carved furniture of this type which was intended to be gilded or painted.

58

61

61. A French Empire Bird's-Eye Maple Sofa, 1790s

1700-1800

The severe form of this French Empire-period bird's-eye maple sofa originated in the Republican period. Napoleon and his court were influenced by the restraint of earlier design styles, and especially took a great interest in Classical architectural forms. The light-coloured woods, such as maple, which were favoured in Germany were also preferred in France, and the use of flat shapes and curves within a single plane was common to progressive furniture makers in both countries. This version is made with great simplicity and reveals a use of basic shapes and materials suggestive of the much later Bauhaus philosophy.

59

60

62. A Dutch Neo-Classical Mahogany Sofa, c1790–1800

By the closing years of the 18th century, the simplicity of neo-Classical forms, first popularized in France, influenced the design of furniture for middle-class use. In the Low Countries, French influence was especially strong, although the love of ornament for its own sake, rather than to augment the classical inspiration of a piece, was never abandoned completely. This marquetry-decorated mahogany sofa was made in Holland and stands on semicircular moulded bracket feet. In marquetry the ground is a veneer rather than solid wood, making it possible to apply the decoration in a sheet. The favourite woods for use in marquetry were sycamore, plane, holly and poplar, although other light woods were sometimes dyed to give a greater variety of colours. Sofas of this form, but without the inlay, were especially popular in the early years of the 19th century.

63. An English George III Mahogany Sofa with Tapestry Upholstery, c1790–1800

By the last years of the 18th century, sofas and chairs had become much squarer in form. The strength of mahogany was especially suitable for slim, tapered legs. Frequently, the complete back and sides were upholstered, but this version is made more interesting by the front legs, which are extended to form the fronts of the arms. The seat is padded and fringe-decorated. Tapestry was still a much-favoured upholstery material; it was woven in Britain as well as in France.

64. An English George III Sofa, c1795

The design for this late 18th-century English sofa anticipates the simplicity of European post-Revolutionary structures. The intersection of the arms with the long, rectangular back is quite geometric compared to the fluid lines of earlier pieces. The square, tapered legs are continued to form the turned arm supports, a device that became very popular in the early 19th century. It is upholstered in brocade. Damage to replacement upholstery does not affect the value of sofas of this period, as they are usually re-covered to suit a decorative scheme.

64

63

62

1800 TO 1900

The 19th century was a period of experimentation, innovation and often cheap novelty. As new materials and working methods came into general use, manufacturers competed to produce the most arresting designs that would attract the buyers at the newly fashionable department stores and special exhibitions. The cool Classicism of the early 1800s, achieved by individual craftsmen, was soon displaced by a miscellany of short-lived forms, ranging from the elegant 'Japaneseque' to the crude 'Adirondack Rustic' of American country retreats.

In 1828 the first patent for coiled wire springs heralded changes of basic form and structure that were to revolutionize the design of seat furniture. In order to accommodate the springs and cover them adequately with layers of stuffing, seats had to be much deeper, imparting a heavier, less elegant effect. In some mid-19th-century versions, there is no visible show-wood and some frames were even made of iron. Such sofas are usually deep-buttoned and sometimes have additional springs at the back to give the High Victorian overstuffed effect. Unfortunately, many of these completely upholstered versions have been re-covered, thus losing the complexity of the original effect, a look that was achieved by the use of figured velvets, brocade, plush or tapestry, trimmed with fringes and tassels.

One of the greatest influences on British and American design in the early 19th century was Thomas Hope, whose *Household Furniture and Interior Decoration*, published in 1807, popularized Egyptian and Greek forms. In his Moorish-style drawing room he used massive sofas that were continued around corners and finished with impressive sphinxes to emphasize the Eastern theme. A more formal sofa, with sabre legs, was finished off by a frieze containing the twelve great gods of the Greeks and Romans. Other sofa designs were copies of marble sarcophagi whose original austere effect disappeared under bright red, green or yellow upholstery and the bronze Eastern or classical emblems that decorated the plainer mahogany. Hope's designs were imitated in a much simplified form by cabinetmakers, who sometimes superimposed his ornament on much cheaper structures to create a somewhat tawdry effect. In the 1830s, AWN Pugin led a Gothic Revival movement, away from ornamental Classicism and back to what he believed were the only true styles, firmly rooted in ecclesiastical tradition. He also advocated the use of natural materials, a philosophy that was constantly expounded by John Ruskin, the influential writer and critic. The romantic medieval idealism of these men was perpetuated by William Morris and other exponents of the Arts and Crafts Movement, who attempted to improve the taste and behaviour of society by designing and producing handsome furniture and textiles intended for daily use.

As standards of living improved, craftsmen and factory workers also developed a pride and interest in their homes and purchased small sofas for their front parlours. To satisfy this new mass market, a cheaper type of furniture began to appear. These sofas were produced by the busy furniture factories that gradually were replacing the small workshops in the old tradition. By 1900 this new industry was making thousands of identical couches, daybeds and suites. Such furniture was often flimsy and covered with cheap fabric that soon needed replacing.

The 19th century was also characterized by the rise of the big furniture warehouses and department stores where sofas were well displayed, sometimes in handsome settings. Indeed, shopping had become a more pleasurable occupation and the displays encouraged people to take an interest in decoration, an interest that was fostered by the many magazines and books available on the subject. Many of the writers suggested the use of antique sofas, a taste that the factories satisfied with a proliferation of reproductions in the Queen Anne or Jacobean style.

The great international exhibitions of the mid-19th century inspired manufacturers to produce the most highly ornamented and extravagant sofas that could possibly be contrived. Many of these showpieces were not intended for normal commercial sale, but to exhibit the skill of the manufacturer to the judges. The work of Indian, Japanese and Middle Eastern craftsmen was also brought to the attention of the public by such events.

In the United States, lavishly ornamented sofas in the Rococo Revival style were especial favourites, imparting as they did an atmosphere of great luxury. John Henry Belter, a German émigré working in New York, was to become the great commercial exploiter of the idiom. He combined technology with fanciful designs by patenting a method of laminating thin layers of wood so they could be steam-moulded. Working in a completely different style, Michael Thonet of Vienna also experimented with laminating techniques, producing some of the most progressive bentwood designs of the period for the mass market. Thonet chaises longues, two- and three-seater sofas in adult and child sizes, and hall and veranda settles all poured across the world, the lightness of their construction making them cheap and easy to transport.

Some of the most decorative Victorian sofas were made by an even earlier, though far less durable, process of lamination. Indeed, papier-mâché was already popular before its success at the Great Exhibition of 1851 in London. Made from pulped paper, glue and often sand that have been moulded and baked, Victorian papier-mâché was painted, gilded and inlaid with mother-of-pearl on a rich, usually black, ground, thus providing a highly dramatic effect. As significant parts of their structures were fragile, relatively few papier-mâché sofas have survived, so that any extant example in good condition attracts a high price, especially if its maker is known.

Such excesses of ornamentation and the increasing use of machine carving caused a number of craftsmen to revolt and start up various reform movements in Europe and North America. The best-known sofas in the idiom are the sturdy oak settles by Gustav Stickley's Craftsman Workshops in upstate New York and the high-backed versions created by William Morris and his British followers, who also popularized 'Cosy Corners', sofas that were custom-made to fit the two sides of corners. Such pieces sometimes incorporated a high shelf for books or the display of china.

Fortunately, most 19th-century sofas were strongly made and a sufficient number appear on the market to give the buyer a wide choice. Most popular are the cabriole-legged chaise longue and the many variations on the double-ended spoon-back form with attractive show-wood. So popular are some of these mid-Victorian designs that they are being reproduced today. By 1900 a move towards simpler designs had begun, although such progressive pieces remained the province of a small group of artists, intellectuals and wealthy, discerning people – very much the same clientele that the Morris group had attracted. Most factories and cabinetmakers continued to produce heavily padded furniture alongside reproductions of 18th-century designs, so that furniture catalogues and magazines of the 1890s show sofas in a much wider assortment of styles than are available today.

65. An English Neo-Classical Sofa, designed by Thomas Hope, c1800

Thomas Hope (1769–1831) designed this sofa for his house in Duchess Street, London, which he acquired in 1789 and decorated in mainly Greek Classical style. The sofa was intended for the 'Lararium', one of the most curious rooms in the house, which contained Egyptian, Hindu and Chinese idols and curiosities and which was strewn with cotton drapery to give a tented effect. The sofa has a frieze that depicts the 12 great gods of the Greeks and Romans as represented in, in Hope' own words, 'The old stiff style of workmanship, round the Bocca di pozzo, in the Capitol'. Hope opened his Duchess Street house to the public and his designs were imitated widely, although in a much less ornamented and eccentric style. The design for the sofa was published in 1807.

66. A Russian Neo-Classical Mahogany Sofa, c1800

Little Russian furniture appears on the international market, mainly because the finest houses were decorated with French and Italian pieces. This example, made around 1800, is in the neo-Classical style and is brass-mounted. The lattice-panelled back gives the sofa an air of lightness and simplicity, characteristic of the early 19th-century interior. Made of mahogany, it stands on square, tapering legs, headed by roundels and joined by stretchers – the latter a necessary feature of such a delicate construction.

67. A French Consulate Mahogany Chaise Longue, attributed to Jacob Frères, c1800

Made c1800, this mahogany chaise longue is a superb example of the new classically styled furniture design that emerged after the French Revolution. Attributed to Jacob Frères, it was originally part of a salon suite and has shaped rectangular out-curved open sides with turned and tapered lotus-carved crest rails. The rectangular moulded splat is carved with a lozenge that encloses a central mask of Mercury and four paterae, each carved with a perched griffin and berried anthemion, one of the most popular early 19th-century motifs. It has a loose, rectangular cushion seat above a conforming seat rail, It is fitted with a panelled demilune, or half-moon, apron carved with a mask of Apollo. Dating from the Consulate period (1799–1804), the chaise longue stands on tensed animal legs with paw feet. The Jacob brothers made many of the pieces for the Empress Joséphine while she was furnishing Malmaison.

68. An American Early Federal Inlaid Mahogany Sofa, c1800

This inlaid mahogany sofa was made c1800 in New York. Pieces such as this in classical Federal style are highly coveted and command top prices. A most elegant piece, the sofa has an attractive, slightly bowed seat covered with a loose cushion. It stands on line- and bellflower-inlaid square, tapering legs, ending in cross-branded cuffs. The term 'Federal' is a chronological and not stylistic one, used for American furniture made between 1790 and 1830. It is so called because this was the period of Federalist-Party rule in Washington. The Federal style in American furniture is based mainly on late 18th-century European designs, although Federal pieces often have less ornamentation.

69. An American Early Federal Sofa, c1800

America's Federal Constitution, signed in 1787, fostered an even greater awareness of national pride and identity. The new nation favoured a Classicism that was restrained and very elegant, and any sofas in the style are now highly prized. The design of this piece, with its canework panels, is typical of the turn of the century, when the use of ornament was still firmly controlled. The shallow carving of the back rail is typical of the period, as is the use of unadorned but beautifully worked and finished wood.

65

67

66

69

68

1800-1900

70. A French(?) Empire Walnut Day-Bed, after 1800

Day-beds of this type first became popular in France and were copied in other countries throughout the 19th century; they are still made today, although mainly for use in bedrooms. This walnut example has a prettily carved frame with the decorative addition of swags of carved leaves and flowers to the seat rail. Similar designs were produced in the last quarter of the 18th century, but the outward splay of the legs suggests a date after 1800. This type of day-bed was a progression from the separate armchair and matching stool of which Chippendale was so critical. More recent examples have sprung seats with a separate feather-filled squab cushion for added luxury.

71. An American Early Federal Mahogany Sofa, attributed to Samuel McIntire, c1805

This simple carved-mahogany sofa, was made in the United States c1805. The shaped back rail has carved and punch-work decoration comprising clustered fruit and flowers with swags centring four arrows. The arms are carved with acanthus, and the bowed seat is supported on square tapering legs. The carving is attributed to Samuel McIntire (1757–1811) of Salem, Massachusetts, as it has identical elements to the decoration on a documented McIntire piece in the Museum of Fine Arts, Boston.

72. A French(?) Ormolu and Mahogany Sofa, c1810

Ornately decorated with ormolu mounts, this small two-seater sofa is probably French, dating to c1810. It has a mahogany frame, and the seat rail features a rope-carved motif, centred with an ormolu pendant of leaf form. The back rail is also carved with linked flower forms, with an ormolu mount of crossed arrows in the middle. Acanthus-leaf ormolu mounts are featured, as well as bosses and ormolu on the legs. Such a piece, with its shallow buttoning and its rather over-fussy appearance, was popular with the new bourgeoisie of the First Empire.

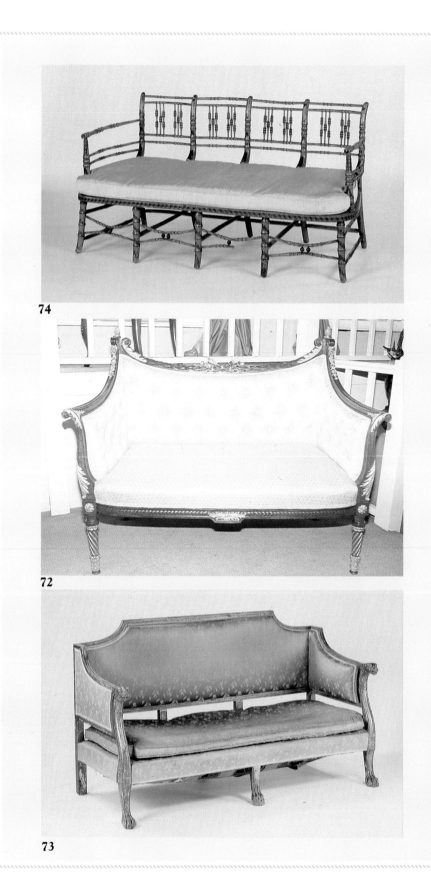

74

72

73

73. An English Regency Gilt-Wood Sofa, c1810

In this Regency gilt-wood sofa, the severity of the rectangular back is broken by the curved sides. The arm supports, surmounted by animal heads and ending in paw feet, suggest a French influence. The sprung seat was a later addition. Originally the squab cushion would have rested on a padded surface. Styles from different countries were adopted much more quickly in the 19th century, with many European craftsmen taking their skills far afield.

74. An English Regency Quadruple Chair-Back Simulated-Bamboo Sofa, c1810

The ten legs of this English Regency-period four-seater or quadruple, chair-back sofa are united by plain and turned stretchers. An unusually complex piece, it is made of simulated bamboo. In 1803, Thomas Sheraton had described how beech was turned in imitation of bamboo, and the taste for such faux-bamboo was continued to some extent throughout the 19th century. It was a great favourite in Regency England, especially for the furnishing of interiors in the chinoiserie taste; such pieces were frequently painted or gilded.

71

70

75. An English Regency Parcel-Gilt and Oak Sofa, attributed to George Bullock, *c*1810

Deep fringes were often used in the early 19th century to decorate the lower edge of sofas, but were removed in the mid-20th century, when such ornament was felt to clutter the basic line of a piece. This oak and parcel-gilt example is of especially fine quality and is attributed to George Bullock (1777/8–1818), who worked out of Liverpool and London and furnished some of the most important houses of the period with his expensively constructed pieces. Some of Bullock's finest furniture was made of oak, and he was particularly fond of the use of inlays, roundels and turned, tapered legs. Bullock worked in the fashionable tastes of his time, including Gothic, but his most recognizable pieces are in the rectangular Regency style. Sofas of this quality were usually sold complete with loose protective covers of damask chintz or brown calico.

76. An English Regency Rosewood Sofa, *c*1810

The strong, rectangular shapes of English late 18th-century sofas were developed into a more pronounced and exaggerated form during the Regency period. Plain but highly polished back rails accentuated the line. The seat rail, often covered by the upholstery fabric in the previous century, was now revealed, again to emphasize the sofa's geometric structure. This rosewood version stands on fluted baluster legs, the show-wood continuing on the fronts of the arms. The slightly softer English approach can be seen in the rounded legs and the carving on the arms. Sofas of this type remained popular for use in libraries and other 'masculine' rooms until the 1870s.

77. An English Regency Triple Chair-Back Ebonized-Wood Sofa, *c*1815

A fine example of an early 19th-century English triple chair-back sofa, this piece stands on turned legs. The back rails have painted decoration and are separated by trellis-work back rests. The sofa has an ebonized finish and is very much in accord with the Regency taste for a variety of paint effects. Gold on ebony was a special favourite, particularly in the United States, where the combination was used on country-made pieces decorated by itinerant craftsmen.

77

79

78

78. An English Regency Quadruple Chair-Back Parcel-Gilt and Ebonized-Wood Sofa, *c*1815

This simple version of a Regency-period quadruple chair-back sofa reveals the importance of turning in furniture that was being made in greater quantity for the rapidly expanding middle classes. The ebonized and parcel-gilt sofa has a particularly pleasing back rest, although the lower section is in part spoiled by the complexity of stretchers and legs that form the necessary support for this type of structure. The seats of such sofas were often caned, which made them a little more comfortable.

79. An English Regency Ormolu and Mahogany Low Sofa, *c*1815

The simplicity of some of the more progressive Regency designs suggests a much later period, so much so that this low sofa would fit equally well in a period or modern setting. Made of mahogany, the sofa features ormolu mounts, and the seat is centred with a delicate formal motif. The rich colour of mahogany provided an excellent foil for ormolu, while its strength allowed it to be inlaid and carved. Fairly low Regency sofas are popular for use in modern drawing rooms, where the higher, more Germanic versions appear much too formal.

75

76

1800-1900

80. An American Empire-Style Mahogany and Canework Sofa, *c*1815

The most progressive elements of European design were combined in New York to produce this mahogany sofa in a cool and reasoned interpretation of the Empire style. Made *c*1815, the back rail is carved in low relief to provide just enough ornamentation to soften the classical line. The method of constructing the leg supports is highly functional and made the piece of furniture very strong, despite its linear, quite delicate effect. The use of caned panels instead of upholstery contributes to the light but handsome styling. The addition of lion-paw feet is an acknowledgement of the European influences on American design and was added as a conventional rather than an intrinsic element.

81. An English Late Georgian Gilt-Wood Sofa, *c*1820

Although a number of such sofas were originally painted, relatively few have survived in good condition. The Prince Regent had made decorated furniture more acceptable in Britain by his interiors at the Royal Pavilion in Brighton, where paint and gilding were often combined. This elegant sofa, made *c*1820, reveals the lasting strength of the classical movement, especially in the shaping of the back rail. The low scrolled end is a particularly pleasing feature of this example. The carved headrest and the cabriole legs are gilded for greater effect. This piece is an unusual form of a basic design more commonly found in mahogany. Most sofas of this type are fitted with a mattress that is either tufted or buttoned. It is this type of 19th-century furniture which first became collectible, particularly in North America, where it began to be used in fashionable interiors in the 1930s.

82

80

82. An American Neo-Classical Mahogany Sofa, attributed to Duncan Phyfe, c1820

1800-1900

This fine neo-Classical mahogany sofa has been attributed to Duncan Phyfe (1768–1854) and was made c1820. Phyfe, Scottish by birth, was listed in New York City directories from 1792. The line of this sofa is not as pleasing as his best work, although the use of classical motifs on the legs is typical of the fashion for Greek- and Roman-inspired devices, especially popular in New York between 1805 and 1825. Phyfe specialized in light, very elegant seat furniture, usually made of mahogany, a wood that was strong but had a good, rich colour. In Phyfe's workshops different craftsmen were responsible for various aspects of a piece's construction and assembly, a prototype of sorts of later factory methods. The moulding on the front rail is typical of the personal style Phyfe developed from English Regency designs.

83. An English Regency White-Painted and Gilt-Wood Sofa, 1820–30

This sofa is typically 19th century in construction, but was made very much in the grand manner of the early 1700s as part of a suite for an important house. Dating to the reign of George IV (1820–30), the low, rectangular padded back supports three cushions. The seat rail is continued upwards to the outward-splayed arms, which hold the long squab mattress in position. The heavy spiral-turned legs are an unusual feature. The structure is painted white and gilded, and the seat rail is decorated with gilded flower motifs.

81

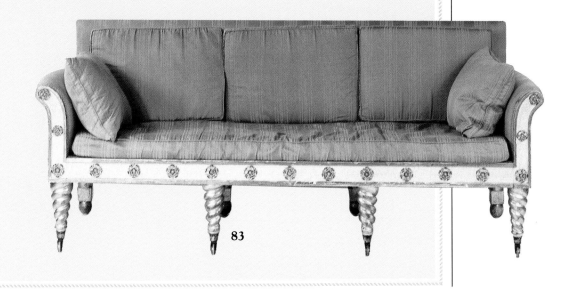

83

84. An English Gothic-Revival Rosewood Sofa, c1825

In High Gothic style, this sofa, with its dangerous-looking pinnacles, is the type of structure that was often criticized by the high priest of the taste, architect AWN Pugin. The aim of many furniture makers who worked in the style was to create pieces that resembled the more ornate early Gothic buildings, admired because of their ecclesiastical grandeur. Made during the reign of George IV and dating to c1825, this triple chair-back version is made of rosewood inlaid with satinwood stringing. The ogee-arched backs are bordered with pierced strapwork and the fluted pinnacle supports are also pierced. The padded arms are decorated with a carved foliate scroll, and the concave-shaped apron is decorated with unusual tracery. The structure stands on tapered legs ending in square feet.

85. An English(?) Late Regency Rosewood Sofa, c1825–35

Rosewood was very popular in the second quarter of the 19th century, especially for the show-wood on drawing-room and parlour sofas. The very simple square lines of this sofa are somewhat in the Beidermeier idiom, although the piece is probably English, as indicated by the carving of the show-wood and the baluster-turned legs. Intended to stand against a wall, this type of sofa was suited to the more formal social uses of the late Regency period. The back has shallow buttoning, and the arms are upholstered in a manner suggesting the styles of the Victorian period.

86. An English Regency Parcel-Gilt and Simulated-Rosewood Sofa, c1830–37

Large suites of furniture in much lighter construction were popular in the drawing rooms of the Regency period. Such furniture was designed to display the simple grace of the occupant and the cool elegance of the fashionable interior, rather than for comfort. This sofa, in parcel gilt and simulated rosewood, comes from a suite comprising a sofa and six open armchairs. The quadruple back provided useful seating for a number of people in the much smaller reception rooms of town houses of the period. Caned seats made it possible to move the furniture much more easily, at the same time contributing to the then fashionable light and delicate effect. The trellis-work back and the turning of the front legs show a slight influence of the chinoiserie taste.

85

86

1800-1900

87. An English Regency Rosewood Chaise Longue with Brass Inlay, *c*1830–37

A nicely proportioned classical example of the Regency period, this chaise longue is made of rosewood, one of the most popular woods of the time, and is inlaid with brass, another highly favoured form of decoration. The inlay on the seat rail is generously detailed, and there is additional ornamentation on the outward-curving legs. These comfortable day-beds were intended to be moved about the room, for example, from fireside to window, and usually have castors. Although used in the 18th century, castors are much more common on 19th-century sofas. In this instance the metal mounts on the feet are original and contribute to the classically inspired effect. The original upholstery was probably silk or damask, although most sofas of this period have been reupholstered a number of times.

88. A German Biedermeier Maple Sofa

A classic and very fine example of the Biedermeier style, this maple sofa is one of a pair. The term 'Biedermeier' derives from the German word *bieder*, meaning plain and unpretentious, and it was a style with its roots in middle-class taste. The sofa was one of the most important items of furniture in the German house, and a sofa of this superb quality, made of very expensive wood, would have been made for wealthy people. The shaping of the arms is both unusual and skilful, as the round bolster fits within the curve. The use of inlay is characteristically delicate and was intended not to intrude on the simplicity of the basic design.

89. An English Late Regency Mahogany Sofa, *c*1835

Exhibiting a strong German influence, this sofa, made *c*1835, shows some lingering elements of the Germanic Biedermeier style, especially in the flat arm fronts and the geometric shaping of the seat. The purity of the German styling of the sofa, which was in fact made in Britain during the reign of William IV, is submerged in ornament, in order to create a more impressive piece of furniture for homes where wealth had to be displayed. The detachable back has pierced foliate cresting centred by a scallop shell. The vase-shaped arm facings are decorated with foliate scrolls, and the apron is carved with anthemia. The mahogany sofa stands on carved, shaped feet.

91

90. A French Mahogany Day-Bed, *c*1840

A nicely shaped *meridienne*, or day-bed, this mahogany sofa dates to *c*1840. Such pieces first became popular in France during the Napoleonic period. This version has a shaped padded back and scroll arms within a plain frame showing a strong Biedermeier influence. The scrolled arms are in the softer style that generally became popular in the second quarter of the 19th century. The moulded arms and the deep apron are decorated with applied gilt-metal leaves and swags. The *meridienne* stands on well-shaped scroll feet. The foot of such a day-bed can sometimes be lowered to give added length, although in this example the section is fixed in position,.

91. An English Victorian Rosewood Sofa, *c*1840–50

This massive and ornate early Victorian sofa is now reupholstered in red brocade. Made of rosewood, it stands on heavily carved cabriole legs ending in realistic ball-and-claw feet. The simplicity of the seat and back rail shows the ongoing influence of early 19th-century forms, although, in this instance, the styles look satisfactory together. The curved wooden arms reveal a more progressive influence. One of a pair, the sofa was probably made for a ballroom or a very large drawing room. Originally, there were probably some matching armchairs.

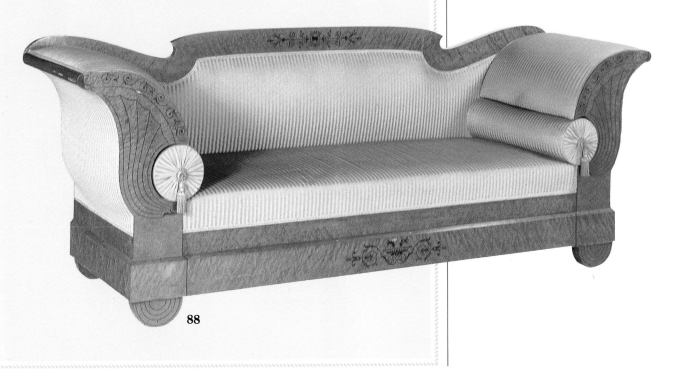

88

92. An English Victorian Georgian-Revival Sofa, *c*1840s

A mid-19th-century English-made sofa, this example is in the impressive, somewhat heavy style especially preferred for use in dining rooms and libraries. The shaped back can be taken off, thus allowing the piece to be moved more easily. The short, sturdy cabriole legs and the deep carving of the apron below the seat rail make the design typical of the 1840s, when flat shapes or massive turned legs were more common. Variations on this heavy style of English furniture continued to be made until the 1920s in Eastern countries such as China and India.

93. A French 19th-Century Gilt-Wood Sofa in Louis XV Style

French furniture makers have always had a fondness for sofas with padded oval backs. In this 19th-century gilt-wood version in Louis XV style, the oval is part of the back rail, which has a moulded leaf-carved frame with beaded edging. The scroll arms are leaf-carved and have small, padded armrests. The sofa stands on spirally fluted, leaf-carved turned legs. There is a separate padded cushion. The sofa is from a salon suite that also includes six matching armchairs.

94. A French Louis XVI-Revival Sofa, *c*1850

During the 19th century French furniture makers constantly produced retrospective designs. This piece was in the style of the 1780s, although it was constructed *c*1850. Standing on tapered legs, the gilded sofa has a moulded frame and upholstered arm supports. When reupholstered in a sympathetic fabric or in one of the French machine-made tapestries popular for such revivalist pieces, the structure would have much greater appeal. Similar designs have been produced in France throughout this century and can often only be precisely dated when the original covering is intact.

96

92

95

95. An English Mid-Victorian Upholstered Chaise Longue/Settee, 1850s

Some sofas were a combination of a chaise longue and a double-ended settee. Two people were able to sit comfortably on this overstuffed version. The inward curve of the seat is especially attractive, as are the boldly shaped feet. Such designs, whose upholstery was fixed to a wood or even metal framework, were much more economical to produce than those with an abundance of carving or inlay. The introduction of coiled springs made seats much more comfortable and it is this aspect of many 1850s sofas that gives them so much appeal today. This example was reupholstered in the 1930s in an unsympathetic patterned moquette. When re-covered in a more suitable fabric, it will be an attractive decorative piece.

96. A German Rosewood Suite, c1850–60

German furniture, although heavily influenced by French designs, was more restrained in effect. This mid-19th-century suite of neat furniture is made of rosewood and is now upholstered in brocade. The complete suite also included eight side chairs and would have furnished a complete room. The sofa stands on rather poorly formed cabriole legs, but has an attractively constructed seat with a treble curve reflecting the shape of the armchair fronts. The three sections of the apron are carved with the same foliate design that is used for the cresting of the back rail.

94

93

97. Two English Victorian Sofas, c1853

These two designs for sofas come from the *Victorian Cabinetmaker's Assistant*, published in 1853. Such seat furniture was suggested as ideal for the dining room or the library. Both examples stand on turned legs that are continued into the scrolled arms. The top design has the back rest separately applied. The carved ornament on the centre of the front rail is composed of two pieces, joined vertically in the centre and indented. In the upper design the elbow scrolls were clamped onto a hardwood ground and then dowelled on to the legs; the centre ornament of the back was formed from one piece of wood that was mitred on to the moulding and then dowelled in position. Elegant mid-Victorian designs of this kind remain good sellers, although their length – some were intended to seat four people – often limits their use.

98. An English Victorian Sofa Design, 1853

A mid-19th-century progression of an 18th-century design can be seen in this drawing of a sofa, whose basic rectangular line is softened by curved corners. The seat is square-framed and the back was separately applied, this latter device especially useful for large pieces of furniture, which were often difficult to move from the smaller rooms of the period. The moulding on the back rail and the centre of the seat rail was intended to be separately applied, the dark lines indicating where an inlay was to be used. This design for a dining-room sofa was published in 1853 and illustrates how the spare lines of Regency furniture were adapted very gradually for the taste of the middle classes.

99. An English Victorian Sofa Design, 1853

In this 1853 design from the *Victorian Cabinetmaker's Assistant*, the serpentine back rest and the decorative use of buttoning give this sofa a quintessential Victorian look. The spiral pillar and front foot are made from one piece, but the scrolled cap of the pillar was separately carved and then dowelled on. The back of the sofa would have been pegged in position, so it could be taken apart before moving it. Somewhat formal in appearance, the sofa was intended for use in a dining room.

97

99

98

100. Two English Victorian Renaissance-Revival Sofas, *c*1853

Most mid-19th-century sofas of this type have the backs separately fixed, usually with some form of metal bolt. These designs, first published in 1853 in the *Victorian Cabinetmaker's Assistant*, are in the highly ornamented Victorian Renaissance style with impressive crests on the back rails and pendant carving on the scrolled arms. Detail such as the hanging decoration was dowelled in place. These designs could be made of rosewood or mahogany; where rosewood was used, the veneer was applied more thinly and the recessed and delicate parts of the carving could be hatched in gold or gilt. In the top design, the centre of the back, extending to the curve of the moulding beyond the leafage, is made from one solid piece of wood that was 3 in (76 mm) thick. The ring surrounding the head could be turned and later fixed in place and the ornaments on its edge could be shaped on the lathe and then profiled. The head was separately carved and screwed on from behind.

101. An English Victorian Walnut Chaise Longue, *c*1855

An attractively shaped piece, this chaise longue dates to the mid-19th century. It is made of carved walnut and stands on cabriole legs. In the French style, the sofa is from a salon suite comprising a low-seated armchair, an occasional chair, six salon chairs and a pair of footstools. The design of the chaise longue relies completely on the use of curved, organic forms, a style much admired throughout Europe by 1850. The undulating back rail is headed by a carved central motif that is reflected in the decoration of the curved seat rail. In France, similar suites were often gilded, a taste that was never very popular in Britain and North America, where polished walnut or mahogany was preferred.

102. An English Victorian Rosewood Sofa, *c*1855

A good-quality Victorian sofa, from *c*1855, its serpentine back is framed in rosewood. The scroll-end arms have upholstered rests, and the cabriole supports have scroll feet. There is foliate carving on both the arm fronts and the centre of the back rest. It is reupholstered in a striped brocade which, unfortunately, detracts from the attractive shaping of the piece. However, the show-wood on this example has remained in surprisingly perfect condition and adds considerably to its appeal and value.

103

100

100

103. An English Mid-Victorian Walnut Chaise Longue, c1855

An attractive Victorian chaise longue of c1855, this walnut example stands on very cursive cabriole legs. The seat rail is centred with a carved device, the scrolled front arm is also carved and the back rest is deep-buttoned. Now upholstered in moss-green velvet, the piece would originally have been used in a parlour or a very formal bedroom or boudoir.

104. A French Ormolu-Mounted Chaise Longue, c1852–70

At its most ostentatious, some French mid-19th-century furniture seems to have been designed more for a stage set than domestic use. This regal piece was made during the reign of Napoleon III (1852–70), a period characterized by the lavish display of dress and furnishing encouraged by the court. This chaise longue has a rectangular out-scrolled back and a deep, well-padded seat. The sides are decorated with ormolu mounts representing flower- and fruit-filled cornucopias. These are surmounted with a profile of a classical woman and end in rams' heads. The base is centrally mounted with a rectangular plaque depicting various Muses and decorated with scrolling foliage flanked by centaurs and putti. The foot is mounted with a figure of a swan amid scrolling laurel. The chaise longue stands on winged-lion monopodia.

1800-1900

105. A French Boulle Revivalist Sofa, c1860

The seat of this c1860 French sofa has a deep shaped apron front, and its top rail has decoration at the centre. Its appeal, however, lies in its boulle finish. Boulle is an inlay of tortoiseshell, wood and brass that was used by André-Charles Boulle (1642–1732), who was *ébéniste* to Louis XIV. Various methods of laying the thin tortoiseshell and brass on to the wooden carcase were employed . Sometimes the brass, laid on a ground of shell, was engraved or combined with other materials – such as pewter or mother-of-pearl – to create very rich patterns. Boulle marquetry was usually applied over oak or deal, and the parts not decorated with inlay were veneered in a complementary shade of wood. Although the method went out of fashion after the reign of Louis XVI, some pieces continued to be made afterwards, producing an effect both rich and eye-catching.

106. A French Ebonized-Wood and Ormolu-Mounted Sofa, c1860

Dating to c1860, this French sofa is ebonized and decorated with ormolu mounts. Standing on four front and three back legs, the design is unusual in its asymmetry. The high back is also exceptional for the period, and either refers back to 18th-century designs or looks forward to later Art Nouveau. Such a piece would have been made for a very fashion-conscious customer. The use of ormolu was particularly popular with French furniture makers, who embellished their better examples with mounts carved mainly with foliate forms. Although now upholstered with a rather unsympathetic fabric, it would find a ready buyer because of its unusual shape and good general quality.

107. An English Victorian Walnut Sofa, c1860

This Victorian sofa is supplied with scrolls and curves in such abundance that it would satisfy the most ardent lovers of the ornate style. The padded, triple-seat back is set within a pierced, moulded scroll frame that separates to form unusual inverted-heart shapes. The carved apron is centred by a feather motif repeated in a simplified form between the three back supports. It stands on moulded scrolled, curvilinear supports. Made of walnut, the piece was constructed c1860 and would have been used in a formal drawing room, probably along with matching armchairs. Reception-room furniture of this kind was upholstered in velvet, brocade, silk or black horsehair and edged with gimp.

108

107

108. An American Rococo Revival Laminated-Rosewood Suite, attributed to John Henry Belter, *c*1860

John Henry Belter (1804–63), a German émigré working in New York, created innovative pieces in the Rococo Revival style. This suite is made of laminated rosewood, a process he patented. His third patent, registered in 1858, related to seat furniture. Thin layers of wood were glued together and bent under steam pressure in moulds. The resulting thin, curved pieces could then be carved or pierced. He sold his 'Parlour Sofas' in 1855 for $350. This sofa is typical of his work, with its lavish use of scrolls and pierced work in the bold, robust form that was his hallmark. Belter had served his apprenticeship in Germany and the European influence is apparent in his work, although the finished designs are completely idiosyncratic with their hand-carved ornamentation and complex shapes.

105

106

1800-1900

109. An American Rococo Revival Laminated-Wood Love Seat, attributed to John Henry Belter, c1860

The love seat – intended, of course, for two – was especially popular in the United States, with variations produced by many factories. This fine example is attributed to John Henry Belter, although it should be noted that, to date, no piece of seat furniture bearing his label has been found and there were no pattern-books issued by his firm to help in identification. The love seat has his characteristic cabriole legs and a serpentine front to the seat. The use of laminated wood with pierced work and hand carving is also typical of his finest work. Belter Rococo Revival furniture again became popular in the 1920s, and his pieces are today great favourites in salerooms because of the current preference for High Victorian styles. Love seats are especially favoured because they are small enough to be used in a bedroom or a hall.

110. An English Mid-Victorian Carved and Upholstered Sofa, 1860s

This very elaborate sofa exhibits all the features that were scorned in the middle years of the 20th century. Today such pieces are highly desirable and command good prices – despite the very high cost to reupholster them in the original manner. Such designs were most popular in the 1860s when they were covered in richly coloured silks and velvets. In this version, the front of the seat is left plain and edged with cord and gimp. The oval section at the back has a different edging. Such designs required very highly skilled upholsterers, as the shell-like effect of the overstuffed arms would be a problem to all but the most experienced worker. This sofa is especially attractive because of the pierced-work carving on the back and on the seat rail.

111. An English Victorian Sofa, c1860–70

This sofa is a mid-Victorian British interpretation of an earlier French design. The advent of the coiled spring meant that seat furniture could be much more comfortable and they were used even in designs where they were not appropriate, such as this one. The squared seat edged with cord was a popular upholstery of the period, but is only occasionally re-created today when re-covering Victorian furniture because of the additional expense. This type of sofa is very popular, since it combines comfort with a High Victorian effect.

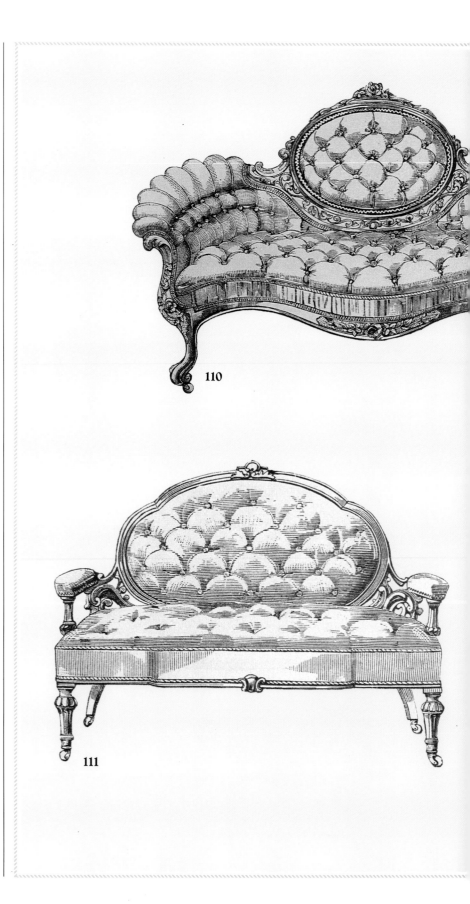

110

111

109

112. An English Arts & Crafts Sussex-Type Settle by Morris & Co, after 1865

The most famous of all the furniture produced by William Morris and his associates was the Sussex type of rush-seated chairs and sofas. Such items were sold by Morris & Co from 1865 until the early years of the 20th century, and they became very fashionable among followers of the Arts & Crafts Movement, as well as those decorating in the Aesthetic taste. The somewhat fragile construction was usually ebonized, but examples were also made in walnut and mahogany. Similar settles were made by several other firms, as they could be produced cheaply enough to supply all sections of the market. Despite the fact that they were not comfortable, these settles were originally intended for use in the drawing room, sometimes accompanied by occasional chairs and armchairs. Today they are more often found in dining rooms or halls.

113. An English Mid-Victorian Walnut Sofa, c1865–75

The attractive shaping of the back of this walnut sofa makes it desirable to anyone furnishing a room in the mid-Victorian manner. Though primarily intended for one person to recline on in the parlour or drawing room, provision was made to seat a second person by rounding and padding the foot. Standing on cabriole legs that continue into scrolled arms, the piece typifies the most decorative furniture of the period made in Britain for middle-class homes.

114. An English George II-Style Walnut Sofa with Needlepoint Upholstery, probably 19th century

As 18th-century sofas in fairly simple styles have been favourites with interior decorators for such a long time, there are many examples extant that have been much restored or slightly adapted. This colourful model, in George II style, is partially composed of 18th-century elements. The walnut cabriole legs have conventional shell carving on the knees and end in ball-and-claw feet. The serpentine cresting above the padded back sweeps to the less satisfactory padded out-scrolled sides. The gros- and petit-point needlework is an especially attractive feature and depicts on several panels a series of figures in Arcadian dress in romantic landscapes. The upholstery is finished with braid and close nailing.

115. An English George II-Style Mahogany and Parcel-Gilt Day-Bed

This day-bed, in George II style, is made of mahogany and parcel-gilt. It has a pierced and carved apron below the gilt Greek key pattern of the seat rail. The cabriole legs end in lion-paw feet, Benjamin Goodison (d.1767) supplied two day-beds of this design for the picture gallery at Longford Castle in Wiltshire in 1740, although these were equipped with a graduated pile of cushions at the head and foot. Fine 18th-century designs have never gone out of fashion completely, and many superb copies were made in the 19th century, when the quality of craftsmanship was still attainable and the knowledge of old working methods still at hand.

116. A French Boulle and Ormolu Revivalist Sofa, c1870

This French-made sofa dates to around 1870, but is made in the style of the late 18th century. Such an impressive revivalist piece reveals the skill of the *ébéniste* to full advantage and would have been very expensive when made, as its surface was finished with boulle marquetry. As boulle was, by nature, fragile, it was usually fitted with ormolu mounts which, besides being decorative, protected the corners and more exposed sections of a piece. The application of ormolu often became an end in itself, with fully gilt sections frequently used for their decorative value rather than practical necessity.

112

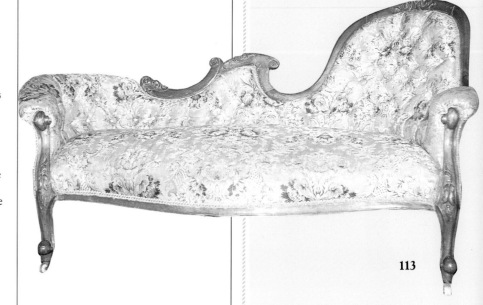

113

116

115

114

117. An English Victorian Curved Sofa by Hampton & Sons, *c*1870

A much more lavish interpretation of a High Victorian curved sofa; such a piece was popular for use in a bay window. Some very large half-round versions were especially made to fit inside windows of that type. The deep buttoning, fringe and ornamental tassels of the overstuffed back all contribute to a piece of furniture that would have been relatively expensive when first produced. Hamptons, established in 1830, included this design in their catalogue of 'Cabinet Furniture', which also stated that their upholstery department was 'composed of English, French and German cutters-out and stuffers, therefore they are enabled for style and taste to compete with any house in the trade'.

118. A French 19th-Century Gilt-Wood Sofa in Louis XVI Style, *c*1870

This gilt-wood sofa is from a French Louis XVI-style suite constructed in the 19th century. The acanthus-carved arms, with padded rests, continue to the delicate stop-fluted legs. The sofa retains its original Aubusson tapestry, which depicts two animal scenes with dogs, birds and serpents set within double borders. The manufacture of tapestry at Aubusson was helped during the reign of Louis XV, when pastoral scenes and landscapes were most popular. In the 19th century, coverings for sofas were produced in quantity, although pieces in good condition are in short supply today. Aubusson tapestry was made for a wide, middle-class market rather than for palaces, and the subjects have a restrained, though charming, quality.

119

117

74

120

118

119. Three English Victorian Upholstered Sofas by Hampton & Sons, *c*1870

It is only in catalogue drawings or contemporary paintings that the complexity of Victorian upholstery can be fully appreciated. The chaise longue in the centre of this page, from the catalogue of Hampton & Sons, London, reveals the craft at its most extreme. The wooden-framed sofa, standing on both turned and cabriole legs, was embellished with a deep fringe terminating in silk drops. As though the back rest was not sufficiently complex, a large wood silk-wound drop gave the finishing touch. The central plain panel, running the length of the chaise longue, was edged with braid and contrasted with the deep-buttoning of the remainder of the seat and the arms. A wider braid was used above the seat rail. Such work was very labour-intensive and obviously expensive but, unfortunately, such pieces have rarely survived intact. The top sofa is of a much more conventional form, although few modern upholsterers would consider deep-butttoning a striped fabric, which is a highly specialized skill whose final result must be perfect. The other example illustrated, a deeply sprung chaise longue, was upholstered in plain velvet or silk and edged with a very deep fringe that concealed its turned legs. Large tassels hang from roundels on its sides and back.

120. An English Victorian Sofa by Hampton & Sons, *c*1870

This is one of the most ornate – and impractical – forms created by the Victorians; the fragility inherent in such a design has meant that few examples have survived. The deep-buttoned upholstered chair backs are joined by a pierced and carved section which gave the piece a charming delicacy but must have been extremely uncomfortable. The complexity of the ornamentation on the back is complemented by the plainly upholstered seat and armrests. An armchair and an occasional chair were made to match this piece, although all were sold separately by London's Hampton & Sons around 1870.

121. An English Victorian Sofa by Hampton & Sons, *c*1870

A somewhat cumbersome Victorian design, this piece of furniture seems to present an excuse for the extremes of the upholsterer's craft. Offered for sale by London's Hampton & Sons *c*1870, the sofa has a shaped wooden back rail and a wooden centrepiece on the overstuffed back rest. It stands on cabriole legs and has a slightly curved seat rail. The customer was able to select the wood for the construction, although stock lines were usually of mahogany or walnut. The cost would have depended mainly on the quality of the covering fabric.

122. Three English Victorian Upholstered Sofas by Hampton & Sons, *c*1870

This trio of sofas was offered by Hampton & Sons of Pall Mall East, London, *c*1870. All rely on the luxurious effect of deep-buttoning and stand on heavy turned legs fitted with castors. The first two designs are typical of the mid-19th century, but the straight-backed settee shows the prevailing influence of Regency-period styles. The central sofa is a curious combination of a settee and a chaise longue, although it would only have seated one person comfortably. Manufacturers such as Hamptons strove to provide the novelty-seeking public with endless variations of the fashionable shapes of the period, adding scrolls, tassels and deep-buttoning to catch the attention of even the most jaded eye.

123. An English Victorian Sofa, *c*1870

An almost monumental sofa, this English-manufactured piece dates to 1870. Many curious designs, which seem to owe as much to the builder as to the carpenter, were made after the 1851 Great Exhibition. Most of the decorative woodwork on this sofa was machine-made, but nonetheless it combines to create a very impressive effect. The contrast of the deep-buttoned and plain upholstery is also striking. A matching armchair and an occasional chair were also available. Today, the cost of upholstering such a sofa in the original manner would be close to prohibitive, so when they appear on the market they are usually plainly covered in velvet, with not even the deep-buttoning reproduced. To result in an effective look, however, the extravagant use of fabric and actual craftsmanship should be copied , thus giving an authentic period atmosphere to a piece.

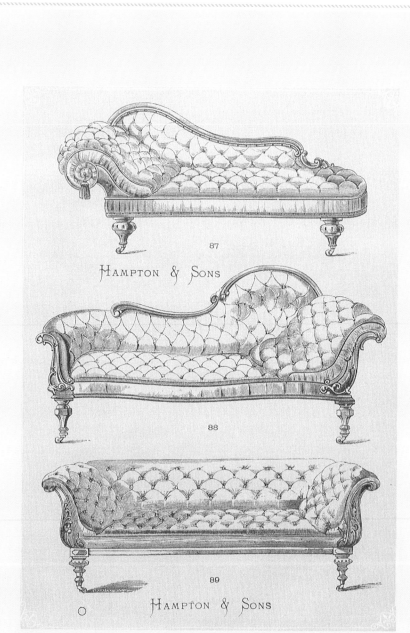

HAMPTON & SONS

HAMPTON & SONS

122

121

123

124. An English Victorian Sofa by Hampton & Sons, c1870

This was one of the most economical styles of sofa offered by Hampton & Sons, London, c1870. It is only the elegant carving of the front of the back rest that separates this design from the thousands that were made for use in working-class homes. The style of the upholstery was very simple and could be replaced by any local handyman. This up-market version relies on beaded mouldings and fluted turned rails for its effect. It was available with an armchair and an occasional chair; such suites were sometimes found in the dining room or study.

125. Three English Victorian 'Conversation' Sofas by Hampton & Sons, c1870

Sofas of the 'conversation' or 'sociable' type were ideal centrepieces in large halls or ballrooms, as well as in the drawing room. In the lower versions shown, no show-wood was visible and the pieces are very much in the manner of Eastern ottomans made without back rests. Such designs relied on the quality of the upholstery fabric, usually silk or velvet, for their effect. In order to give a more luxurious effect, the legs were covered with a rich, deep fringe. The top design was very adaptable although, unfortunately, the occasional chairs and sofas have often been separated over the years and the design of the chairs is not at all satisfactory in isolation. This form of 'sociable' was preferred in France and gilded versions are found more frequently than walnut or mahogany examples. The illustration is from Hampton & Sons' catalogue, c1870.

127

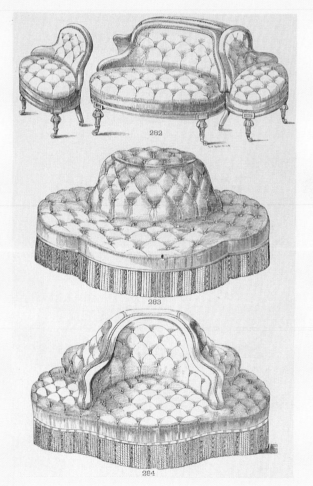

282

283

284

125

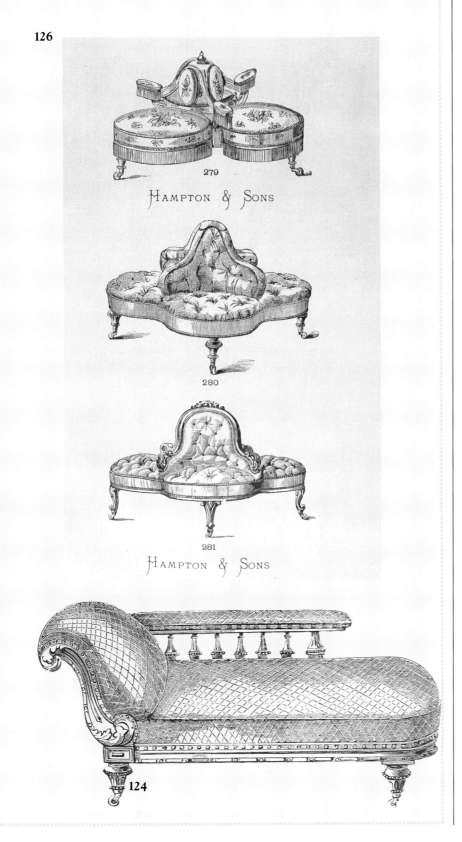

126. Three English Victorian Sofas by Hampton & Sons, c1870

Because of their large size and the high cost of reupholstering, many sofas of this type did not survive the 1930s and 1940s, when they were scorned as examples of the worst excesses of Victorian taste. As relatively few now come on the market, they are much sought after and command good prices. These three models, advertised by Hampton & Sons, London, c1870, show how the structures could be arranged to sit three or four people. The top version is the most extreme; its upholstered armrests on shaped wooden supports would have suffered damage very quickly. This type of upholstery also necessitated custom-woven fabric that would have added to the expense. To give an even greater air of extravagance, deep fringing was used both on the armrests and on the seat. The centre 'conversation' is completely upholstered and deep-buttoned, possibly over an iron frame; it stands on turned wooden legs. The cabriole-legged design is also deep-buttoned, but the structure relies on the show-wood for its effect, making this type of sofa the most desirable – and expensive – today.

127. An English Mid-Victorian Upholstered Sofa, 1870s

It is often only in contemporary line drawings that the finishing detail of upholstery can be seen. This straight-backed sofa, dating to the 1870s, was finished at the lower edge of the seat with a thick cord. A finer version was used to accentuate the square side of the seat, a feature that contrasted well with the deep-buttoning. The construction depends on the use of turned legs and supports, which are also used as part of the decoration. The shaped back rail is centred with a floral crest. The sofa formed part of a suite, along with a matching armchair and so-called 'lady chair' or 'sewing chair', made without arms.

1800-1900

128. An English Victorian Gilt-Wood Sofa, 1870s

One of a pair of English gilt-wood sofas, this example was made in the French manner and dates to the 1870s. Standing on foliate-carved cabriole legs, the sofa has a front seat rail that is centred with a shell. The back is divided into three sections so that the necessary supports form part of the decoration; these supports extend down to form the back legs. The top rail is crested with foliate carving.

129. An English Victorian Mahogany Two-Seater Sofa, 1880s

An almost severely plain English mahogany sofa, this two-seater dates to the 1880s. The simple square lines of the piece are relieved only by a slight curve to the seat. The show-wood around the back and the seat are carved with foliate forms, and the arm supports continue down to simple turned legs. Such pieces, originally designed for more occasional use (such as in a music room), were intended to be placed against a wall, and the backs were therefore very plain. The upholstery, which has been replaced, originally would have been in a similar silk brocade, to further add to the impression of lightness.

130. A French Gilt-Wood Suite in Louis XV Style, 1880s

The furniture styles made popular during the reign of Louis XV have frequently been reproduced. This gilt-wood salon suite from the 1880s is upholstered in brocade of a retrospective style; it is composed of a sofa and four armchairs. The sofa has a padded back set within a shaped moulded frame that is carved with a floral cresting. Its seat and elbow rests are padded, its arms moulded and its shaped apron is carved with flowerheads and leaves. The sofa stands on moulded curvilinear supports with scroll feet. Although such sofas are not very comfortable, they are nonetheless liked because of their versatility: they look effective in a hall, bedroom or drawing room.

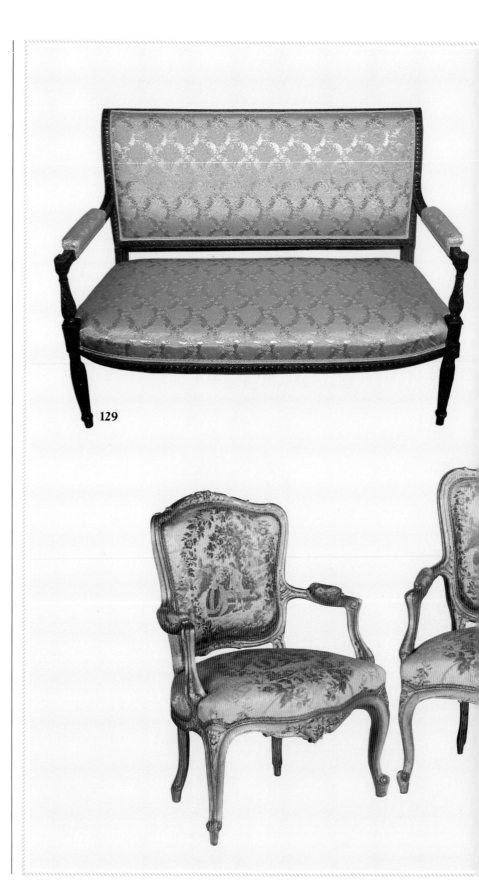

129

128

130

131. A Late 19th-century English Victorian Gilt-Wood Sofa

The best 18th-century designs continued to be reproduced throughout the 19th century, and indeed some are still made today. This gilt-wooden version has a shaped padded back set within a moulded frame, and its border pattern is interspersed with scrolled and foliate devices. The back is surmounted with a very Victorian-style flower and scroll crest. The armrests and the apron of the treble-curved seat front are similarly decorated with moulding. Reupholstered in cut velvet, the sofa also has padded armrests. Traditionally, this type of furniture has not appealed much to British and American buyers, although the market is now widening because of the interest in interior decoration.

132. A French Gilt-Wood Sofa with Tapestry Upholstery in Louis XVI Style, c1880–90

Louix XVI-style salon suites have remained favourites up to the present day and are frequently reproduced. This late 19th-century version, with turned and fluted legs, was probably once part of a suite. The moulded frame is carved with ribbon banding and flowerheads to give the feminine, delicate effect that is typical of the genre. The division of the back into three sections, separated by gilt-wood supports, adds to the light effect of the sofa. During the late 19th century, many reproduction suites of this kind were upholstered with specially woven tapestry panels, often in the 18th-century manner. Also, good-quality silk continued to be used in France for a much longer period than in Great Britain or North America; thus, it can give late sofas a deceptively early appearance.

133. An English Late-Victorian Pub Settle, c1880–90

This late Victorian settle was originally made for a public house in Whitechapel, London. The heavy construction made it ideal for use in an area where the furniture was subject to considerable wear. With its turned legs and rather stiff arms, the piece reveals how traditional designs were perpetuated. Some pub settles have polished wooden seats but others were upholstered in leather or deep plush. Despite their large size, old benches usually sell quickly, as they are preferred for use in hotels. Even in recent years, publicans in London were able to order similarly made pieces from East End craftsmen.

133

132

131

134. An English Victorian Gilt-Wood Sofa in 18th-Century French Style, *c*1880–90

This late 19th-century reproduction of a French 18th-century sofa is now upholstered in flowered cut velvet. The moulded frame has foliate decoration on the back rail, centred with a carved flower device, a design repeated on the two sections of the seat rail. The arms are fitted with padded elbow rests. Gilded French-style furniture of this type has remained popular to the present time and modern reproductions are still made. Victorian versions are favoured because of their high quality.

135. An English Victorian Sofa in William & Mary Style, *c*1885

The popularity of early English furniture is long established and many well-made copies and reproductions of 17th- and 18th-century pieces are now so old that they have a value of their own. Many Victorian-era copies are now appreciated for the quality of their workmanship and, more especially, for the good tapestry, usually French-made, used for their upholstery. As Victorian women also worked on sets of needlework covers for antique-style sofas, it is possible to create a William & Mary-style interior from later, but nonetheless, fine-quality copies. This sofa has well-carved stretchers made of walnut and is decorated with a deep fringe in the late 17th-century manner.

136. An English Arts & Crafts Sofa by Morris & Co, *c*1889

William Morris (1834–96) opened his establishment for the manufacture and sale of household furnishings in 1863. He believed in a return to medieval-style craftsmanship and in making products that should be available to all sections of society; in fact, his creations remained too expensive for the majority. This settle, whose design is attributed to George Jack, was custom-made by Morris & Co for Stanmore Hall in Middlesex; it was one of four intended for the vestibule. Morris & Co was commissioned by William Knox d'Arcy to redecorate and furnish the Hall, to which WR Lethaby also contributed designs. The sofa has a rectangular buttoned back and a fringed padded seat. Its three front legs are spirally fluted and joined by moulded stretchers. The visible wood is mahogany, and the settle is covered with a Morris fabric known as 'Flower Garden'.

137. A Scottish Art Nouveau Settle and Armchair, by Graham Morton, *c*1895–1900

This small high-backed settle and matching armchair were made in a restrained Art Nouveau style in the late 1890s by Graham Morton of Stirling. Light furniture with a limited use of upholstery was preferred by progressive decorators who were reacting against overstuffed Victorian suites. Like the furniture made by Morton's compatriot, Charles Rennie Mackintosh, sofas with such elongated straight backs were not comfortable; thus clients furnishing in the style were generally more concerned with line and fashionable elegance. The craftsmen-made piece is beautifully balanced and ornamented but much cheaper versions in simplified forms were produced at the time by factories. For a sofa in this manner to be valuable, it would need to be attributable to a known maker or a particular school or studio workshop.

136

135

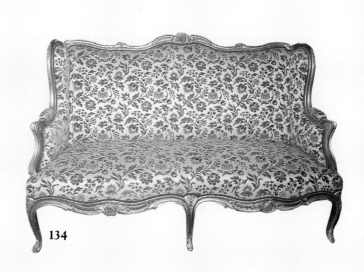

134

137

1900
TO
1999

SITTING ROOM

The industrialization of design has remained the predominant force in popular furniture design of this century. Despite the speed of change, there is a parallel with the development of sofas in the 1800s. Simplicity characterized fashionable pieces in the early years, to be followed by a passion for new materials and methods that were forgotten at the end of the century, when more ornamental seat furniture, often in antique styles, became the vogue. Today, the most expensive sofas have feather-filled cushions and sprung constructions, the antithesis of the avant-garde philosophy of Le Corbusier, Marcel Breuer et al of the 1920s and 1930s. Synthetic upholstery fabrics, plastic preformed cushions and laminated woods are now mainly reserved for cheap mass-produced sofas.

The transition from button-backed sofas with turned legs found in every parlour before World War I, to the Space Age attenuated steel or chrome sculptural works of the 1950s and 1960s, is a reflection of the radical changes and advances in manufacturing methods. Today we have true mass-production with preformed foam padding and simple upholstery that is frequently fixed in position with metal staples. While such production methods have meant that comfortable seat furniture is available to people of all income levels, craftsmanship and the quality of design have suffered, often resulting in dull uniformity. A few exclusive firms do produce finer work, but they often concentrate on traditional styles or reproductions, with exciting sofas seen only in (mostly trade) exhibitions or in the studios of a few innovative craftsmen.

The most desirable 20th-century sofas are made by the well-known progressive designers, whose work set trends that were often modified for the popular market. In the early years, British firms like Heal & Son in London worked very much in the tradition of CFA Voysey and Mackay Hugh Baillie Scott to supply fashionable people with well-made furniture that looked effective in the new-style interiors from which Victorian clutter was banished. Upholstery colours, again in reaction to the dark richness of Victorian rooms, was much lighter, their patterns simpler. Pale greens, cool pinks and fresh lilacs formed a good background for furniture in the high-backed idiom of Scotsman Charles Rennie Mackintosh or the sinuous curves of late Art Nouveau, both styles of which influenced European and American furniture designers well into the 1920s – and have done so again in recent decades.

Alongside early 20th-century designer furniture, which attracted only a small segment of the market, there were many reproductions of 18th-century designs some of which were made to such high standards that they now command good prices. Favourites too were sofas with loose chintz covers, a type that was especially popular for use in the fashionable cottage-style homes that were built in the suburbs as well as the country. Because of its adaptability, chintz-covered seat furniture has never gone completely out of fashion and is currently enjoying another revival.

World War I inhibited the development of European furniture design, but across the Atlantic styles were much livelier. There was a vogue for pale silk-upholstered sofas in plain, rather square designs, a perfect complement for the cigarette-smoking, gramophone-playing fashionables of the early 1920s. Europe caught up with American ideas in the 1920s and strident colours, such as green and red or orange and black, were used for upholstery. Geometric appliqué, tassels and various metallic effects were also applied in the Jazz Age, when the sofa became the centre of a new extravagant lifestyle. Animal-skin covers gave a striking, primitive look to the new metal-framed sofas, while velvet was printed in zebra or leopard patterns.

The progressive functionalism that swept wood aside in favour of manmade materials had its roots in the ideas that had inspired the German Bauhaus, a design school founded in 1919 by Walter Gropius at Weimar. The Bauhaus ideal was to train students in high-quality industrial design that would make use of the new materials for mass-production that were coming on the market. Some of their designs are so rational and timeless that they still appear very modern and continue to influence today's furniture makers. The ideals of the Bauhaus were adapted by well-known designers in constructions that are so famous in the history of design that they are forever associated with their names, such as the beautiful and sculptural chaise longue by Le Corbusier and his associate Charlotte Perriand.

Throughout the 1930s Germans were at the forefront of much of the world's innovative design. The concept of unit seating with sections of the sofa separated with inserts of wood to form tables had been used in Germany even before World War I when fitted furniture began to be popular among the wealthy. By the 1930s birchwood and plywood were often used for sofas, and in Finland Alvar Aalto used laminated wood so skilfully that the arms and backs of sofas were made in one curve. At the San Francisco Golden Gate Exposition in 1939, he exhibited recliners with sculptural laminated sides – a concept that was to influence commercial furniture making across the world.

By the late 1930s, upholstery colours had also become simpler, with creams and brown shades predominating, although abstract patterns, especially wavy lines and triangles, often in cut moquette, were very popular. Such fabrics were often combined with figured walnut that was inset in panels on the arms and occasionally on the backs of the square-look sofas that were found in almost every home. Sometimes a wood-veneered inset was used on the wide arms, to act as a rest for a coffee cup or a cocktail glass. As in collectible furniture from any period, it is the more extreme examples of the style that are most popular today – those seen in glitzy Hollywood films, for example.

Most of the important 20th-century developments in the use of manmade materials for furniture were developed in the 1950s, often as a direct result of experiments that had taken place during World War II. American designers were the most prominent at this time, and were especially active in the field of plastics. Some of the more extreme creations with Space Age insect-like legs made of tubular metal were so uncomfortable that they were made – and kept – for only a short time (making it difficult today to find good examples in the genre). Trendsetting sofa designs created by the likes of Charles Eames are already museum pieces, displayed to represent the great advances in manufacturing methods.

The last quarter of this century is seeing great contrasts of style, ranging from sculptural constructions of artist-craftsmen to pairs of traditionally styled sofas that belong to no particular period. Many of the best designs are directed at the office and contract-furnishing trades; some are modular elements that can be linked to form wall or corner seating. Anyone wishing to invest in the antiques or museum pieces of tomorrow would be well advised to seek out sofas in small craft studios or specialist exhibitions, rather than in the stock of the average furniture shop. Despite the early efforts of William Morris, Charles Lock Eastlake and others who followed in their wakes, the gap between popular and progressive furniture is as wide as ever.

138. An Italian Art Nouveau Banquette by Carlo Bugatti, c1900

Part of a wonderfully exotic drawing-room suite, this is one of the most arresting sofas ever designed. Created by Carlo Bugatti (1855–1940), it combines metallic insets with light and dark woods in a curious Italian interpretation of the Art Nouveau style. Bugatti created a sensation with his eccentric furniture at the Turin Exhibition in 1902. Moorish and Far Eastern influences are often predominant in his designs, and he was willing to combine various materials and techniques in order to create a special effect: polished metals, silks, carved wood and paint, for instance, could be contained in a single piece. This sofa is a superb example of his creative genius at its most extreme, revealing his passion for suspended circles, thonging and massive silk tassels.

139. An English Late Victorian/ Early Edwardian Yew and Elm Sofa in the Windsor Style, c1900

Made c1900, this triple chair-back settle reflects the popularity of antique furniture at the turn of the century. The classic Windsor-style sofa is made of yew and elm woods and has lancet backs with pierced splats. The shaped, solid seat is set on unusual pierced cabriole legs, and the crinoline stretchers are also quite decorative. The Gothic shaping of this George III-style settle makes it especially attractive, particularly in combination with the fine workmanship that it exhibits. Despite being a reproduction, the settle sold at auction for several thousand pounds, revealing the strength of well-made Edwardian reproductions. The term 'Windsor' is used for stick-back chairs with turned legs, solid seats and arms, which were mainly produced in the High Wycombe area of Buckinghamshire from the late 17th century. American Windsors are more usually painted, although those made in Britain and intended for use in the garden were also coloured. They are differentiated by the shaping of the back and can have fan, hoop or comb backs.

140. An English Edwardian Chesterfield Sofa, c1901–10

An Edwardian version of the Victorian Chesterfield, this sofa is now upholstered in Italian damask. In most designs of this type, the arm can be lowered, enabling the user to recline on the sofa. Because of the seat springing and the overstuffed arms, seating of this type was extremely comfortable. Layers of straw, horsehair and padding combined to make furniture that relied for its effect on the quality of the upholstery fabric.

140

138

139

1900-1999

141. A Scottish Art Nouveau Built-In Sofa by Charles Rennie Mackintosh, *c*1902–04

This built-in sofa at Hill House, Dunbartonshire, Scotland, was designed by Charles Rennie Mackintosh (1868–1928), who was also the architect of Hill House. His early work was much influenced by CFA Voysey, but by 1900 his own elongated, dramatically simple styles were well established. As he was primarily an architect, he was mainly interested in furniture that contributed to the totality of a house or room. His built-in seating set new trends which were to have a considerable influence on the development of German commercial furniture. This example is one of his simplest constructions, relying on upholstery for its effect. Much more typical of his work are the decorated cupboard fronts and the high backed occasional chairs. The simplicity of such interiors appealed to the more artistic sections of society and the work of Mackintosh and his Glasgow followers was featured in the leading journals on the Continent.

142. An English Edwardian Chesterfield Sofa, *c*1905

The Victorian Chesterfield-type sofa was updated in the Edwardian period by the addition of a high back, which gave it added comfort. Although the proportions of the Chesterfields were more pleasing to the eye, this new design gave the user more support for his or her back. Standing on solid, turned legs, the sofa had adjustable arms at either end. It was upholstered in a fashionably patterned tapestry.

143. An English Edwardian Sofa in 'Queen Anne' Style, *c*1905

The Edwardian passion for furniture made in 'Queen Anne' style is evident in this high-backed example, which stands on rather long cabriole legs. It is upholstered in Morocco leather and has a sprung seat stuffed with hair. Although such atavistic designs were admired, the comfort of coiled springs was not abandoned in the interest of authenticity.

141

142

143

144

145

144. An English Edwardian Mahogany and Upholstered Sofa, c1905

A simple Edwardian sofa made in Britain around 1905, this stands on sturdy turned legs and features a back rest decorated with machine carving. The sprung seat and heavily padded back rest made the piece quite comfortable and, happily, they have survived in some number. In this example, the show wood is mahogany, but cheaper versions were made on which a heavy stain was used to disguise the construction.

145. An English Edwardian Walnut Suite in 'Queen Anne' Style, c1905–10

By 1910, it had become fashionable to furnish with antiques, although everything made after 1800 was largely ignored. Good 18th-century furniture was scarce, so high-quality copies were produced. Some of these are so good that they now attract very high prices when they appear in the salerooms. This chair-backed sofa, part of an early 20th-century reproduction of a 'Queen Anne' suite, was produced in figured English walnut. Its makers claimed it was a copy of an original at the Victoria and Albert Museum, and it was suggested as furniture for a dining room in the traditional style. The complete suite originally cost £35.

146. An Italian Art Nouveau Sofa, by Ernesto Basile, c1900

This sofa, part of a suite, was designed by the Italian architect Ernesto Basile, who was appointed as chief designer at Vittorio Ducrot's interior design workshop based in Palermo, Sicily, in 1898. Basile's design output for Ducrot was largely in the 'Stile Liberty' (the Italian term for Art Nouveau, coined in tribute to the London department store), combining elegance and function, although he also produced pieces employing the more overt organic forms usually associated with Art Nouveau. Ducrot's firm was on a solid commercial footing, producing quality furniture for hotels and private homes, although some prestigious projects were also commissioned.

147. An American Arts & Crafts Teak Settle, by Charles and Henry Greene, 1906

This teak storage bench was designed by Charles and Henry Greene for the Blacker House in Pasadena, California, in 1906. The two Greene brothers were primarily architects who, upholding the traditions of the Arts & Crafts Movement, believed that the furniture and fittings of a house should be in perfect accord. Like Gustav Stickley, in New York State, they drew on traditional American styles but were prepared to accept modern construction methods much more readily than their British counterparts, they were also influenced by Japanese design. This teak settle, with a carefully constructed but deceptively simple back rest, derives from the functional pieces owned by the early settlers. The seat lifts in two sections for access to the storage space below. In rural homes, this would have been used for linen or blankets, but in the elegant houses of the avant-garde, who commissioned most of the Arts & Crafts work both in the United States and Great Britain, it was more likely to have been used for travelling rugs or the storage of decorative textiles.

149

146

148. An English Edwardian Polished-Mahogany Suite with Tapestry Upholstery, 1909

This type of suite was high fashion in 1909, when very light furniture was used in reaction to the deep-buttoned heavy products the Victorians had loved. The pierced centre splats of the chair and sofa backs show a tentative influence of the Glasgow School. Many painted suites of this design were made, but in this instance polished mahogany, decorated with an inlay, was employed. Tapestry was used for the upholstery.

149. An English Edwardian Sofa, 1909

The Edwardian affection for lighter furniture inspired some designs that now look skimpy. Piped cushions and upholstery became more commonplace after 1920, making this 1909 example progressive, if hardly attractive. Originally it would have been upholstered in plain, ribbed tapestry.

147

148

150. An American Arts & Crafts Oak Hall Bench, *c*1910

Gustav Stickley (1857–1946) was a follower of the writings of William Morris and believed that the design of furniture should evolve in a natural way from the traditions of its country of origin. Working in northern New York State, he was also heavily influenced by the somewhat austere style of Shaker furniture, from which all ornament was banished. He described the pieces he made as 'Structural'. This *c*1910 oak hall bench is typical of his work, for which locally available woods were used in order to make it cheap enough for middle-class Americans to own. Stickley believed that art should be brought into the homes of ordinary people and that by using well-designed objects in daily life they would be encouraged to adopt a plain-living, high-thinking philosophy. The products of Stickley's Craftsman Workshops enjoyed great popularity in the early years of the 20th century, as did his monthly journal, the *Craftsman*. Examples in the early tradition, such as this settle, are very popular, as they typify the American Arts & Crafts movement.

151. An English Arts & Crafts Living Room with Built-in Sofa, designed by M H Baillie Scott, 1911

The influence of William Morris extended into the 20th century because of the strength of the various designers that perpetuated his Arts & Crafts ideals. In this living room, designed by M H Baillie Scott (1865–1945), the sofa is built into an alcove with shelves for the storage of books and ornamental pieces. Created in 1911, this room represents a lighter interpretation of the Arts & Crafts tradition. Baillie Scott favoured painted interiors, wherein furniture and wall decoration combined to give a somewhat medieval atmosphere. Most of his furniture was made of oak or mahogany by JP White of Bedford. Since Baillie Scott's individual furniture pieces were not highly original designs their impact can only be appreciated fully in the designer's drawings, which combine his furniture with carefully selected rugs, murals and fittings.

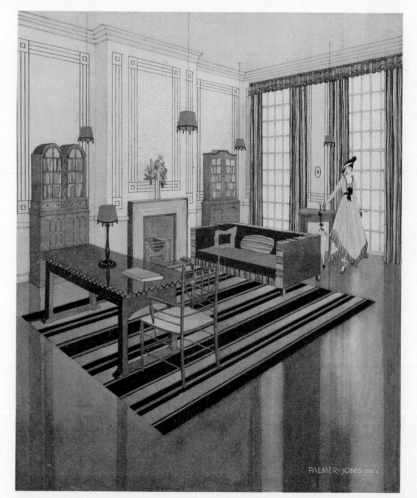

152

150

151

152. An English Sitting Room with German-Style Sofa by Heal & Son, c1918

Heal & Son furnished this fashionable sitting room for a town flat around 1918. The sofa is in the simple German style and composed of plain, flat shapes that were ideal for mass-production; it stands on wooden legs. For its effect it depends on the use of a contrasting fabric that accentuates the angular line. Heals, based in Tottenham Court Road, London, aimed at producing simple but good-quality furniture in which both traditional and modern influences were apparent. Ambrose Heal Jr (1872–1959), joined the family business in 1893 and by 1901, at the Glasgow Exhibition, was well-known for his simple furniture with its reticent use of ornament. Many Heal designs were trendsetters for later mass-producers of furniture. The use of brightly coloured cushions in abstract patterns was to be a common feature of sofas in the 1920s.

1900-1999

153. An English Upholstered Sofa, 1920s

The elegant lines of this sofa are obviously derived from the 18th century, but the lack of any visible show-wood and the fact that the seat continues down to floor level make its 1920s origin perfectly clear. Well constructed and featuring feather-filled cushions, it was marketed as a quality piece in its time. Today it would no doubt find a ready buyer, someone who wishes to obtain classical, well-made and comfortable seat furniture.

154. An English Early 20th-Century Knole Sofa, 1920s

Dating to the 1920s, this is a curious variation on the traditional Knole sofa. In this design the two high sides can be lowered, but the padded arms remain static. As in a genuine Knole, the sides are held in place with ornamental tasselled ropes which are looped around the back projections. The high sides of a Knole made the design especially suitable for use in draughty, cold rooms, while the depth of the seats made it possible to use the structure as an occasional bed. Until recently, such 20th-century examples were almost unsaleable but the current interest in curious, decorative furniture has made them more popular.

155. A French 20th-Century Gilt-Wood Sofa in Louis XV Style

This sofa, upholstered in brocaded silk, is a good 20th-century reproduction of a Louis XV-style piece. The padded back is set within a moulded frame with a foliate scroll carved cresting. The apron is also decorated with a foliate scroll at the front centre and there is further carving on the cabriole legs as well as the arm and back supports. The sofa comes from a five-piece salon suite also comprising two armchairs and two side chairs. Gilt-wood furniture of this type, although constructed comparatively recently, sells for good prices because of the high quality of the workmanship.

153

156. An English Sitting Room with Chesterfield Sofa by Heal & Son, 1920s

A simplification of the Victorian Chesterfield sofa, this example stands on square, tapering feet and is upholstered in the plain fabric that was so fashionable in the early 20th-century. The ruched cushion, seen on the floor, was a type that became very popular in the 1930s and was often found on sofas and armchairs. This sitting room was designed by Ambrose Heal of Heal & Son; the illustration, by Palmer-Jones, is from a contemporary magazine. The stark simplicity of the light fitting and general décor contrasts with the antique-style pie-crust occasional table and the lamp table. The growth of decorating magazines in the 1920s and 1930s made the general public more aware of design trends, with fashions changing at an accelerating rate during these decades.

156

154

155

157. An English Two-Seater Sofa, 1920s

This typical 1920s two-seater sofa has matching cushions on the seat and at the back. Boldly patterned upholstery fabrics, which were in vogue during this period, have again come into fashion. The feather-filled cushions make this design even more luxurious. Cheaper versions were supplied with fillings of cotton waste or even straw.

158. An English Three-Piece Suite, including a Chesterfield Sofa, 1920s

By the mid 1920s, the matching 'Three-piece Suite' was an essential part of every British middle- and working-class home. This type of sofa structure, with comfortable springing and a high back, continued to be made until the 1950s. The maker described this sofa, rather confusingly, as a 'Chesterfield'; the term is now used only for a sofa whose padded back and arms end at one level. This suite was constructed with hardwood frames, and extra-long, steel-coppered springs were said to be used. The pieces stand on round, turned feet. The double-boarded front, emphasized by the use of cord trimming, was a popular design feature of the period.

159. An English Cretonne-Covered Chesterfield Sofa, 1920s

In the 1920s, ordinary working people were able to buy new furniture for their homes. As many of these had small sitting rooms traditional designs, such as the Chesterfield, were adapted for such interiors. This version was deeply padded and well sprung, making it extremely comfortable. One arm could be dropped, so that, despite its length, the sofa could be used for reclining. The basic version was sold covered in plain cotton upholstery. The illustrated model has a loose cretonne cover.

160. An English Oak Convertible Sofa, 1920s

The concept of a sofa that converts into an occasional bed has great practical appeal, and examples from the 18th and early 19th centuries occasionally appear on the market. This advertisement for 'A real friend in need' appeared in the 1920s. Made of turned wood, the sofa was 45 in (115 cm) wide and pulled down to form a full-length bed. The finish was described as 'Jacobean Oak'. It was fitted with corduroy cushions available in four colours. At just under £3, it must have been one of the cheapest pieces of furniture on the market. For an extra 10 shillings a full double-bed width was available.

Price for COMPLETE SUITE
£17 : 10 : 0
60/- with order
58/- balance monthly.
Full cash with order
£16 : 12 : 6
WRITE NOW FOR PATTERNS and select your own coverings.
SENT POST FREE

158

157

159

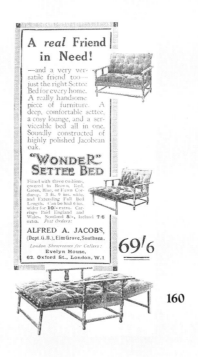

A *real* Friend in Need!

—and a very versatile friend too—just the right Settee Bed for every home. A really handsome piece of furniture. A deep, comfortable settee, a cosy lounge, and a serviceable bed all in one. Soundly constructed of highly polished Jacobean oak.

"WONDER" SETTEE BED

Fitted with three cushions, covered in Brown, Red, Green, Blue, or Fawn Corduroy. 3 ft. 9 ins. wide, and Extending Full Bed Length. Can be had 6 ins. wider for **10/-** extra. Carriage Paid England and Wales. Scotland **5/-**, Ireland **7/6** extra. *Post Orders:*

ALFRED A. JACOBS,
(Dept. G.H.), Elm Grove, Southsea.

London Showrooms for Callers:
Evelyn House,
62, Oxford St., London, W.1

69/6

160

161. An English Built-In Sofa, in Cottage Tudor Style, featured in 1922 advertisement

In the early 20th century, the window-seat sofa became a great favourite for the country cottage-type suburban house, often in the Tudor style that was sprouting throughout Britain. Functional wooden frames were produced, which could be extended to fit a bay of almost any length. The effect depended completely upon the attractiveness of the upholstery fabric. This advertisement for 'art furnishing' dates from 1922, but the style had been used by artistic people before 1900. As sofas of this type were built-in, very few have survived intact.

162. An English Carved-Rosewood Settle in Chinese Style, 1924

The current passion for decorative furniture has popularized 19th- and early 20th-century Oriental furniture, which formerly was extremely difficult to sell. An example such as this would always have attracted some attention, as it is both cleverly made and has a known provenance. It is marked with two metal and enamel commemorative medallion insets, surmounted by flags and bearing the inscription: 'British Empire Exhibition 1924, Chinese Restaurant'. The pierced and carved back is ornamented with a fruiting-vine motif and has a central upholstered splat. Made of 'Huang hua-li' wood, a Southeast Asian rosewood, the settle's panelled seat has scrolled ends, made more comfortable with a squab cushion. The settle has a pierced and carved ornamental apron at the seat front and stands on cabriole legs. Pieces made for the great international exhibitions were always of good quality, as they functioned as advertisements for the products of the various countries.

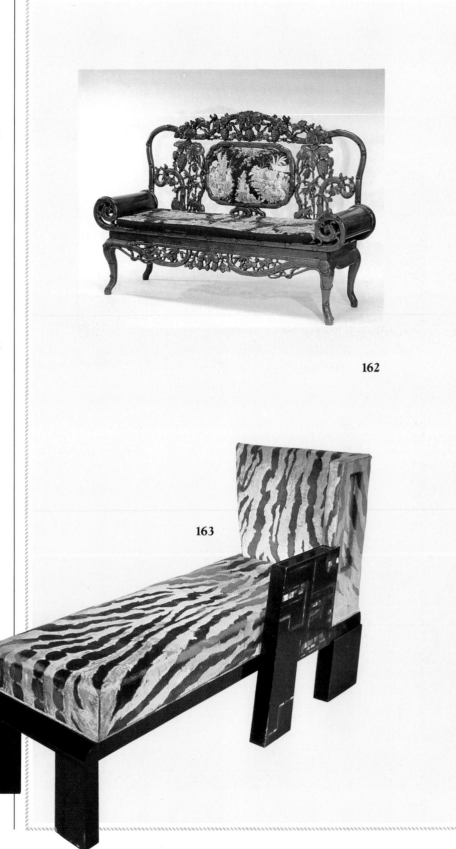

162

163

163. A French Art Deco Lacquered Chaise Longue by Pierre Legrain, 1925

One of the most famous 20th-century sofas is this chaise longue designed by Pierre Legrain (1889–1929) in 1925. Legrain was typical of several versatile Art Deco designers in Paris who could create almost any object from a chair to a scent bottle. Like Carlo Bugatti in Milan, he was fascinated by exotic materials and forms. The chaise longue reveals his quirky, capricious approach, as the 'zebra' skin in fact is made of soft printed velvet and the armrest, usually placed against a wall (and consequently invisible) is beautifully decorated with mother-of-pearl. There is a small shelf at the front of the armrest, perhaps for an elegant cigarette holder or a slim volume of avant-garde poetry. Although its structure looks very simple, almost crude, the sofa is beautifully finished, making it an exotic and expensive fancy.

164. A French Art Deco Smoking Room by Jean Dunand, featuring a Lacquered Settle, 1925

In this smoking room with lacquered walls, ceilings and fittings, a modern sofa is seen at its most basic. Designed by Jean Dunand, who was especially fond of lacquered effects, this bench-type settle was made for the Pavillon d'un Ambassadeur, exhibited at the 1925 Paris Exposition. It depends for its effect on the abstract upholstery fabric, although the basic construction is extremely simple. Such completely functional pieces of French Art Deco furniture contrast with the highly decorated pieces which designers like Dunand, Marcel Coard and Pierre Legrain also made. For collectors of vintage furniture, the period is especially interesting as, even in the work of one designer, the contradictory influences of northern Europe, Japan and Hollywood can be seen.

164

161

165. A French Art Deco Gilt-Wood Suite by Louis Süe and André Mare of the Compagnie des Arts Français, c1925

This sofa, with its matching armchairs and footstools, is part of a seven-piece suite designed by Louis Süe (1875–1968) and André Mare (1885–1932), which was especially made for the 1925 *Exposition Internationale des Arts Décoratifs et Industriels Modernes* in Paris. The tapestry upholstery is after Charles Dufresne. The gilt-wood sofa, with its drop-in squab cushion, is deliberately atavistic in style, and is well served by the traditionalism of the tapestry covering. In fact, Süe and Mare often looked to much classic 18th-century French furniture design for their inspiration. Indeed, luxury and comfort were the two most important elements in the design of traditional-style French sofas shown at the Exposition, yet, alongside such suites, pieces in the decidedly progressive Moderne idiom were also displayed.

166. A French Art Deco Gilt-Wood Suite by Maurice Dufrêne, c1925

The strong colours, exotic costumes and opulent stage sets of Diaghilev's Ballets Russes influenced all spheres of French design after the company's triumphal Paris debut in 1909. In this salon suite, the Beauvais-tapestry upholstery has been woven in a painterly, Fauvist style that can almost be considered a distinct homage to the Russian impresario. Its designer, Maurice Dufrêne (1876–1955), worked for the Parisian department store, Galeries Lafayette, which set up La Maîtrise in the 1920s, an atelier for the design and production of furniture and other decorative arts. This gilt-wood sofa is a superb example of a carefully planned, progressively designed piece of decorative furniture relying more on visual impact than function.

167

169

167. A French Art Deco Gilt-Wood Sofa with Tapestry Upholstery, designed by Paul Follot, 1920–25

Much French Art Deco furniture was superbly crafted of often-lavish materials and decorated with a traditional Gallic attention to detail that distinguished it all the more. This sofa, part of a suite of furniture, was designed by Paul Follot (1877–1941), whose influence on the development of French interior decoration between the wars was considerable. The gilt-wood sofa shows a tentative updating of the 19th-century design, and is used in combination with a strikingly modern tapestry upholstery.

168. A French Gilt-Wood Sofa in the Empire Style, c1926

The French love of gilded furniture continued into the 20th century. In this fashionable flat, photographed in 1926, the very tentative influence of the Art Deco style can be seen in the furnishings. The design of the three-seater sofa was described as 'Empire Style'. The dark brown velvet upholstery was chosen to blend with the purple, gold and grey of the other furnishings.

169. An English Moderne-Style Suite, late 1920s

Most mass-produced English furniture of the late 1920s attracts little interest, but this suite, whose forms somewhat relate to the French Art Deco style, is a good example of down-market Moderne. Although the style is at odds with the close nailing of the upholstery, it is sufficiently pronounced to give a good period feel to a decorative scheme. The sofa was upholstered in 'antique' brown Pexine or Pegamoid and fitted with brown velvet cushions. It was sold by the Midland Furniture Galleries, Southampton Row, London.

166

168

165

170. Reproduction of an English Sofa by Sir Edwin Lutyens, 1929

Despite the general decline in craftsmanship after World War II, it was still sometimes possible to obtain work made to very high specifications. This is a recently made sofa constructed from a design by Sir Edwin Lutyens (1869–1944), known as 'the society architect'. This sofa was originally designed for Government House, New Delhi, in 1929 and is a good example of the careful elegance that was a feature of all his work. In the tradition of great architects, Lutyens designed a great deal of furniture to complement his houses.

171. An English Art Deco Chaise Longue by Betty Joel, c1930

The manufacturers of foam-filled furniture embraced the styles of designers such as Betty Joel (b.1896) to create seating where comfort was paramount. This progressive chaise longue was created by Joel c1930. Betty Joel Ltd produced some of the most progressive British furniture of the 1930s and 1940s, making use of steel and laminated wood. In this sofa, padding gives a feeling of luxury to a simple curved shape, making it a desirable item for an interior in the Art Deco style. To some extent, the progressiveness of this structure is lost because of many modern interpretations.

172. An English Two-Seater Sofa by the City Cabinet Works, c1930

During the 1920s and 1930s most ordinary British families owned a sitting-room sofa of this or very similar type. This version, made by the City Cabinet Works in Moorgate, London, was one of the more expensive designs and was upholstered in French damask. A three-seater, 6–ft (1.8–m) version was also available. The sofa had a birchwood frame and coppered steel springs, and a mixture of hair and fibre was used for stuffing the cushions. Like many other sofas of the period, it was available in a fixed or drop-end style.

171

170

172

173. An English Modernist Laminated-Beech and -Plywood Chaise Longue, by Marcel Breuer for Isokon, 1935

Laminated wood was creating considerable interest among furniture makers by the late 1920s, and Marcel Breuer had produced a cantilevered chair in 1925. This chaise longue, in laminated beech and plywood, was designed by Breuer in 1935 for the Isokon furniture company of London. Breuer designed his furniture both in steel and woods, to provide maximum comfort with a minimum use of material and labour. The chaise longue reveals how modern furniture-making methods can be used to create a structure in which perfection of form is still paramount. Breuer had left his native Germany in the early 1930s to work in Great Britain. He perpetuated many of the ideals of the Bauhaus philosophy, using great economy combined with the most up-to-date methods of construction to create highly sculptural, modernist furniture. This chaise longue was originally fitted with a continuous cushion that did not detract from the concept of unity.

174. An English Painted and Upholstered Sofa by Duncan Grant and Vanessa Bell, mid-1930s

Custom-designed for a music room, this sofa was created by Duncan Grant and Vanessa Bell in the mid-1930s. Its fabric was especially printed to complement the painted murals in its setting, where the furniture was intended not to intrude but to form part of a complete harmony. The painted furniture and the rugs were also designed by these Bloomsbury Group artists. This upholstered, very simple sofa illustrates the very different approach of the artistic avant-garde in the 1930s and 1940s in comparison to the austere work of the leading German designers, who were banishing all superfluous decoration from their creations.

175. 'Mae West Hot Lips Sofa', based on a painting by Salvador Dali, 1936–37

The 'Mae West Hot Lips' sofa designed in 1936–37 by Salvador Dali (1904–89), is a classic example of the way a piece of furniture can be used to express an artistic concept more dramatically than a purely decorative object. The nonpareil 'Cupid's bow' lip shape, popularized by the 1920s and 1930s actresses, offered the artist an organic and highly sexual outline, ideal for a display piece. Upholstered in vibrant red, with the lips slightly parting as the sofa was sat upon, the sexuality of the object is positive and aggressive.

176. An American Model Room containing Plexiglas Furniture by Lorin Jackson, c1940

By 1940, manmade plastics were becoming an important material for furniture making. In this contemporary photograph, the transparent plastic called Plexiglas was used for most of the objects. The substance was mady by Rohm & Haas Co Inc and was used for the chairs, side tables and picture frame, as well as the sofa's arms and legs. The furniture in the room was designed by Lorin Jackson and was exhibited at Grosfield House in New York in 1940, at the annual exhibition of decorators' interiors. Furniture of the type was still very expensive, and it was not until the 1950s that plastic became cheap and widely used. This early use of plastic is interesting, as it shows a sofa made in a progressive material for the luxury trade.

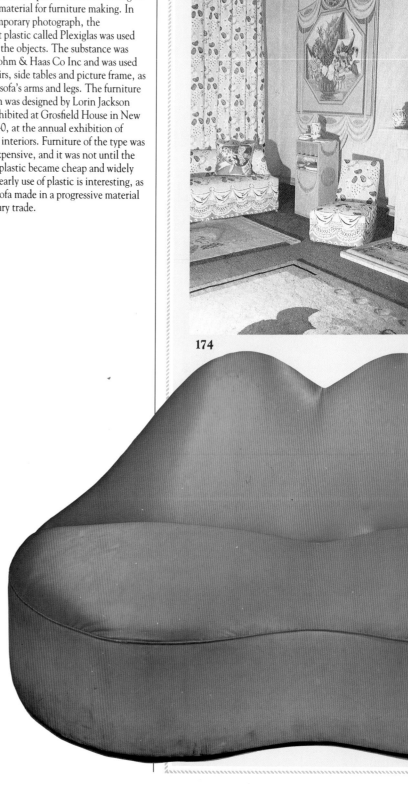

174

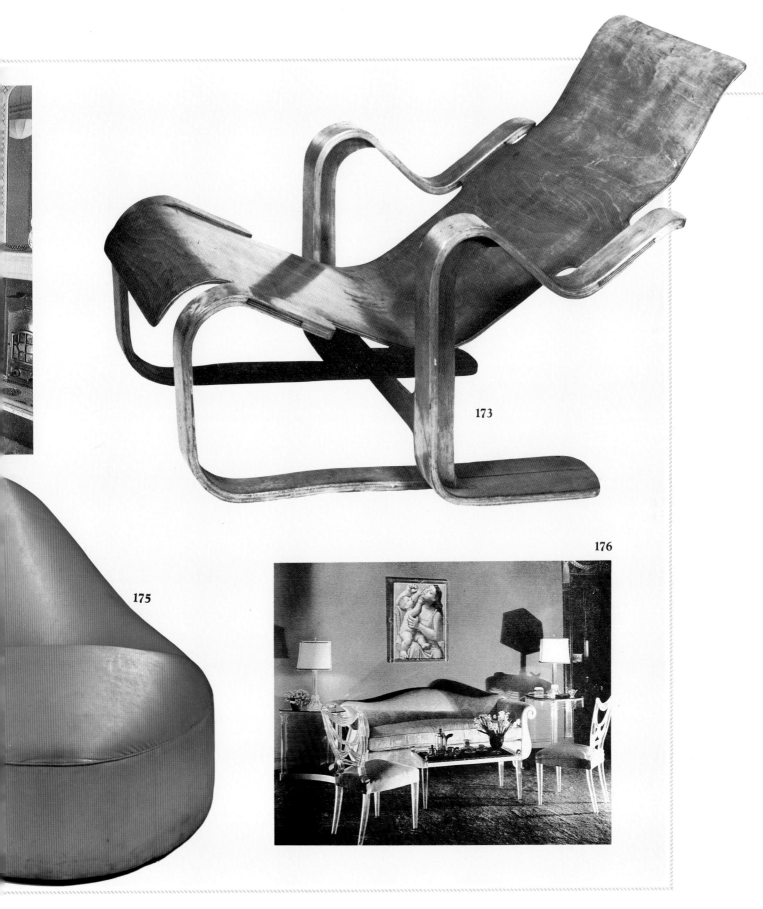

173

175

176

177. An American Interior containing an Upholstered-Wood Sofa, 1940s

American designers led the world in the 1940s, as furniture making in Europe was restricted to pieces in the most economical styles. The sofa is composed of the rectangular shapes that were later to form the basis of many mass-produced pieces in the 1970s; it is upholstered in a blue-green textured fabric. At the fireplace side there is only a soft cushion, but the other arm is upholstered over wood to form a support for the integral shelves that acts as an occasional table. In this Los Angeles interior, the movement away from the suites of seat furniture that were favoured in the 1930s can be seen, as the chairs were upholstered in contrasting colours.

178. An American 'Marshmallow' Sofa by George Nelson for Herman Miller, Inc, 1956

The amusing 'Marshmallow' sofa, dating to 1956, suggests the atmosphere of the period – rock 'n' roll, wasp waists and a passion for wire framework in everything from underwear to furniture. This sofa, with its spindly legs and geometric shapes, heralds the 'Op Art' styles of the early 1960s. Its designer, George Nelson (b.1908), design director of the trendsetting American firm Herman Miller, Inc, from 1947 to 1965, created furniture for the open-plan type of interior that was popular in that period. Tin-lined furniture of this type, with molecular shapes, sometimes in different colours, produces a Sputnik-like effect.

179. An English Pop Art Sofa, 1950s(?)

A Pop Art sofa made in the deliberately bad taste known as 'kitsch', its designer is not known (perhaps by choice!). An Edwardian couch, with machine decoration and standing on turned legs, has been transformed into a work of art by the witty addition of a reclining lady, her breasts forming additional cushions on the back-rest. The sofa is upholstered in gold satin to form the lady's evening dress, and the incised and machine-carved decoration has been highlighted in gold to give further richness. Parts from a shop-window display figure have been adapted to form the 'human' head, arms and feet. Such pieces by known artists are now heavily collected by enthusiasts who specialize in these amusing creations of the 1950s and 1960s. During the latter decade, many curious sofas were made for shops such as Mr Freedom in London, which sold one sofa made as a set of huge false teeth.

177

179

178

1900-1999

180. An American Leather Chaise Longue by Charles Eames, *c*1968

One of the most elegant of modern designs, this sofa is very much in the Bauhaus idiom. It was designed by Charles Eames (1907–78), perhaps the most important 20th-century American designer. This model was especially made *c*1968 for the director Billy Wilder, so he could take short rests during filming. It is typical of the best contemporary furniture, ideally adaptable to any room or environment. In the years after World War II, American designers made great advances in the use of manmade materials and mechanized furniture-making techniques. Through people such as Eames and furniture manufacturers like Herman Miller and Knoll, the philosophy of the Bauhaus became fully realized for the first time.

181. 'Boxing Gloves', a Pair of Italian Leather-Upholstered Chaises Longues by De Sede, late 1970s

The artistic eccentricity of late-1970s furniture is exemplified by this pair of chaises longues. On the borderline between sculpture and furniture, the structures were made by De Sede to form the focal point in any area where they were exhibited. Despite their Pop-Culture appearance, the sofas, leather-upholstered are both comfortable and, in a minimalist setting, very sophisticated. Pieces like 'Boxing Gloves' are, inevitably, of long term interest in terms of the history of furniture design and attract the attention of museums as well as collectors who are buying modern work as investment pieces.

182. An English Library Sofa by Floris van den Broecke, 1979

The sculptural quality of this sofa is clear to see when it is photographed out of doors. It was designed by Floris van den Broecke as a library sofa in 1979 and ranks among the most daring concepts of the period. Using the most up-to-date materials, van den Broecke claims to approach furniture design without any technical or commercial constraints but with a great concern for human scale. Although such a design would be ideally suited to factory production, the conservatism of buyers tends to restrict such structures to an exclusive intellectual market.

183. 'Chairpiece I', An English Plastic Sofa by Floris van den Broecke, 1970–74

'Chairpiece L' reveals modern furniture design at its most elegant. Developed from the organic, moulded shapes that became possible only in the 20th century, such designs could be cheaply mass-produced in plastic materials to provide economical and comfortable seating. Its designer, Floris van den Broecke, described one sofa he created as 'something settled, rigid, enclosed and private'. Another was designed for sleeping, eating, watching television and lovemaking.

182

183

181

180

184. 'Civitas', Seating System by Kurt Ziehmer, 1970s

Modular seating is the most significant 20th-century contribution to the general development of sofa design, providing the versatility that is necessary for both domestic and commercial use. This system, known as 'Civitas', was designed by Kurt Ziehmer, who specializes in seating units. Ziehmer also uses leather skilfully, avoiding the seams that often spoil the effect of the upholstery.

185. An English Seating System by Floris van den Broecke, 1988

This seating arrangement is a development of the brilliantly coloured 'Vis-à-Vis' form of seating, designed by Floris van den Broecke, who was born in Holland in 1945. He both designs and makes furniture and, with Peter Wheeler and Jane Dillon, formed the partnership 'Furniture Designers' in London in 1985. This highly adaptable form of seating is ideal for large areas, such as airport lounges or student common rooms, as it provides lively colour juxtapositions even when the room is empty of people. In use, the elements can be drawn together or widely separated without an interior becoming the visual mess that too often results when ill-assorted group seating is moved about.

186. An English Late 20th-Century Leather-Covered Chesterfield Sofa, 1980s

Leather-covered Chesterfields were considered the height of luxury in the early 1970s and have continued to be popular for use in commercial buildings and 'masculine' rooms. This 1980s model is deep-buttoned and finished with close nailing. It is fitted with two comfortable squab cushions.

187. 'Westbury', An English Sofa by Gordon Russell, 1980s

A product of the Gordon Russell Design Group, this sofa is part of a modular seating scheme. The soft supportive cushioning makes the sofa suitable for a domestic as well as a commercial environment. Known as the 'Westbury', it is also produced as a sofa-bed. Long sofas can be assembled by using additional single and corner units, arms and cushions. This type of modular seating is popular for island conversation units in large reception areas, or to form a rectangular seating area around a fire in the domestic setting.

187

186

184

185

188. An English Sofa from the 'Longford' Range by Minoc Vernaschi for Gordon Russell, 1980s

Some of the better-designed modern furniture is especially made for office or hotel use, but can look good in a domestic setting as well. This sofa, from the 'Longford' range made by Gordon Russell is available with leather or fabric upholstery. The two- and three-seater versions can be used with matching armchairs to give a total look to an office. Designed by Minoc Vernaschi and using the most modern of upholstery methods, the sofa combines a high degree of comfort with crisp styling.

189. An English Sofa from the 'Segmenta' Range by Gordon Russell, 1980s

The 'Segmenta' range, designed and made by the Gordon Russell Design Group, is mainly intended for the reception areas of commercial interiors. As the emphasis is on comfortable but good, basic design shapes, sofas of this type are an attractive alternative to many of the bland structures found in High Street furniture shops. Corner sections, stools, tables, planters, concave and convex sections are all available in the range, so that a unified look can be given to a small or very large room. Office sofas are sometimes inexpensive in relation to the quality of manufacture and the design concept. It is modular sofas of this basic type that most typify the progressive mainstream style of the last quarter of the 20th century.

190. 'Eastside', An Italian Sofa by Ettore Sottsass for Memphis, 1980s

'Eastside', a beautifully structured sofa, was designed by Ettore Sottsass Jr, born in Austria in 1917 but now an Italian citizen. In this design, the headrests, which too often resemble awkwardly positioned cushions, are a pleasing feature of the composition. The statement they make is emphasized by the use of a contrasting colour. Sottsass is often considered the most outstanding Italian designer of his generation, and was a pioneer of the postwar *ricostruzione*. He is an architect, industrial designer and furniture designer, as well as an artist. For a short period in the 1970s he was involved with an avant-garde Milanese group, Studio Alchymia, designing some curious pieces for their collection. Arguably his most important work has been produced in the 1980s by the Milanese group known as 'Memphis', which Sottsass was instrumental in setting up and for which he has become the leading light.

189

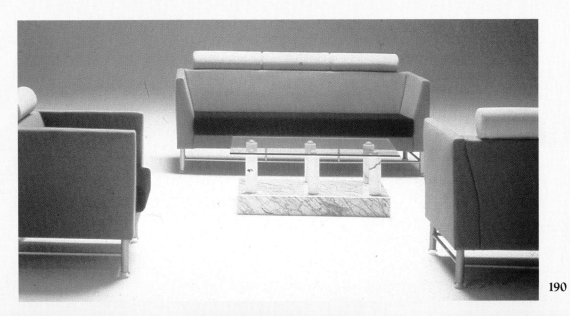

190

188

191. 'The Fakir's Divan', An English Sofa by Danny Lane, 1980s

The fun element that often provides the focus of modern avant-garde furniture is seen in its purest form in this sofa. The traditional chair back form has been amusingly developed to form a structure entitled 'The Fakir's Divan'. Made by Danny Lane, who was born in the United States but now lives in England, it has mobile elements that can be pulled apart and reassembled to make new shapes. This ongoing involvement of the purchaser with the sofa as he or she changes its structure for different rooms or to suit a mood, opens up limitless possibilities for furniture that could be commercially mass-produced from cheaper materials.

192. An English Sofa, 1980s

The simple but classical lines of this sofa make it hard to date it to any particular period of the 20th century, but it is in fact totally modern, although constructed in the traditional manner. No foam has been used in the upholstery, and the seat has spiral springing. The cushions are feather-filled, and the sofa is covered in a Parker and Farr fabric. Such a piece is designed to suit any setting, but because of the method of its construction, it is a necessarily fairly expensive item.

193. An American 'Soft Pad' Sofa by Charles Eames, 1982

Many of the best modern designs look as good in a business environment as they do in a domestic one. This 'Soft Pad' sofa, designed before 1978 but not made until 1982, was Charles Eames's last design. It was structured to give maximum support to the shoulders and head. Eames had originally trained as an architect, but worked with Eero Saarinen on the commercial production of furniture that used modern materials such as aluminium, plastic, fibreglass and plywood. A number of his designs are beacons in the development of modern furniture and have been adapted and mass-produced.

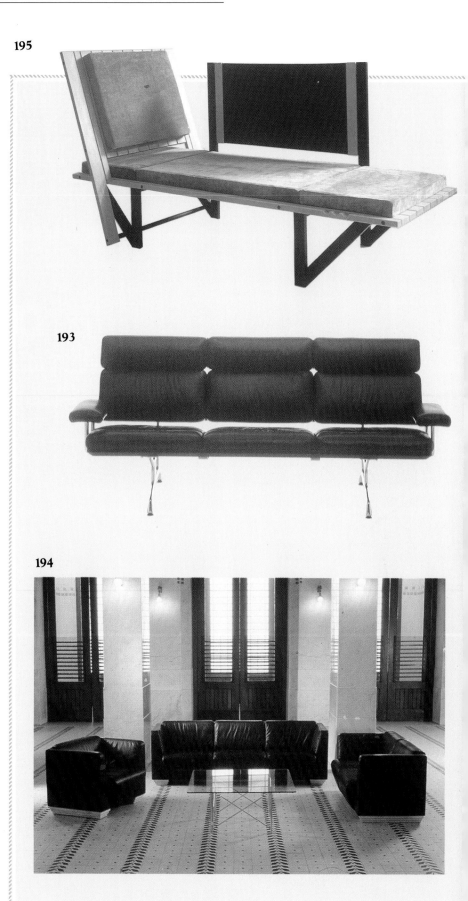

195

193

194

194. A Danish Leather Furniture Suite by Jørgen Kastholm, 1984

A suite of furniture that includes two- and three-seater sofas. This type of unified seating has the adaptability that is necessary both for open-plan living and for contract purchasers. It was designed in 1984 by Jørgen Kastholm (b.1931), whose work has been exhibited at the Louvre in Paris. Kastholm is a university professor and is an architect as well as a furniture designer. This suite is clearly in the northern European idiom and the clean, geometric shapes are combined with good quality basic materials. It is the type of modern furniture that looks well with works of art of any period, as well as with contrasting antique pieces. Kastholm has worked for Fritz Hansen and Ole Hagen and has had his own studio since 1964. The range of objects he has designed includes textiles, light fittings and cutlery.

195. A Chaise Longue by Eric de Graaf, 1984

During the last quarter of the 20th century, the traditional concept of special furniture for specific rooms has disappeared. This 1984 chaise longue by Eric de Graaf, for instance, would look good in a study or a drawing room. The slatted construction and the combination of natural wood with black are reminiscent of the simplicity of Japanese styles. Flat, angular cushions make the sofa comfortable and do not detract from the clean line of the construction.

191

192

196. 'Angaraib', An English Glass and Tree-Branch Chaise Longue by Danny Lane, 1987

An avant-garde interpretation of a primitive Sudanese rope bed, this chaise longue was designed by Danny Lane in 1987. The glass elements, locked into position by their own shape and gravity, float across two parallel branches from a storm-damaged plane tree. This mixture of technology, artistry and conservation is typical of the period, although such structures are as far removed from the lifestyle of ordinary people as the high-style Gothic Revival work of William Burges in the Victorian period. Entitled 'Angaraib', the chaise longue would provide the main focus of attention in any decorative scheme, as well as function as an art object.

197. 'Out of Babylon', An English Glass and Wood Chaise Longue by Danny Lane, 1988

Modern progressive furniture is seen at its most dramatic in this chaise longue entitled 'Out of Babylon'. Made by Danny Lane in 1988, it is a development of an all-glass 'Chaise Longhi' (*sic*) that he had previously made. This structure also incorporates wood in order to soften and humanize the piece. The original glass version had an all-glass bird beak front that has been kept but is now bolted to a winged animal form made of carved plywood and pine slats. Although it would be exciting to see such designs for sale in furniture warehouses and department stores, they have to be considered mainly exhibition pieces, whose appeal is limited to the most artistic or adventurous.

198. 'Vis-à-Vis' An English Sofa by Floris van den Broecke, 1988

This highly functional 'Vis-à-Vis' dates to 1988 and was designed by Floris van den Broecke, who is chairman of the Independent Designers Federation and visiting professor at the Royal College of Art in London. He was originally trained as a painter, and his furniture duly reveals a love of strong colour, combined with an appreciation of the basics of modern industrial design established by the Bauhaus. Van den Broecke is interested in the idea of a product-development centre, where prototypes could be nurtured. Too often, he feels, good ideas are lost because they are not immediately commercial.

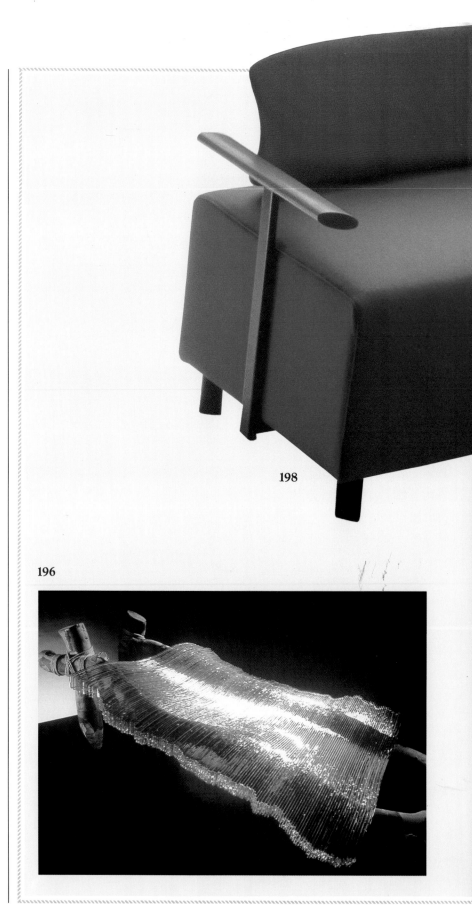

198

196

197

Monarchs

The names of English and French monarchs are often used to denote the period of a piece of furniture when the precise date of manufacture is not known.

In some cases a ruler is closely associated with a recognisable style; Louis XIV, for instance, saw the development of the decorative arts in France as a matter of policy and the massive formal designs of his time reflect the elaboration of life at his court. Dramatic upheavals such as the French Revolution brought about dramatic changes in style but generally changes of style were gradual and overlapped the reigns of different monarchs.

In Britain especially, the machinery of fashion tended to be more loosely linked to the sovereign and public taste was influenced by a variety of factors. This was especially true during the reign of long-lived monarchs like George III (1760-1820) and the names of the producers of cabinetmakers' pattern books, like Chippendale, Sheraton and Hepplewhite are often used quite freely to denote the style of their times. These cabinetmakers were influential not necessarily because of their designs but because they recorded contemporary styles, some of which of course may have been their own.

American furniture periods tend to be classified using a mixture of English monarchs and makers, and the dating is complicated by the fact that it took a long time for European styles to cross the Atlantic so that the American period occurs several years behind the corresponding period in Britain. For example, Queen Anne died in 1714, but the American Queen Anne style is taken to cover the period 1720-1750.

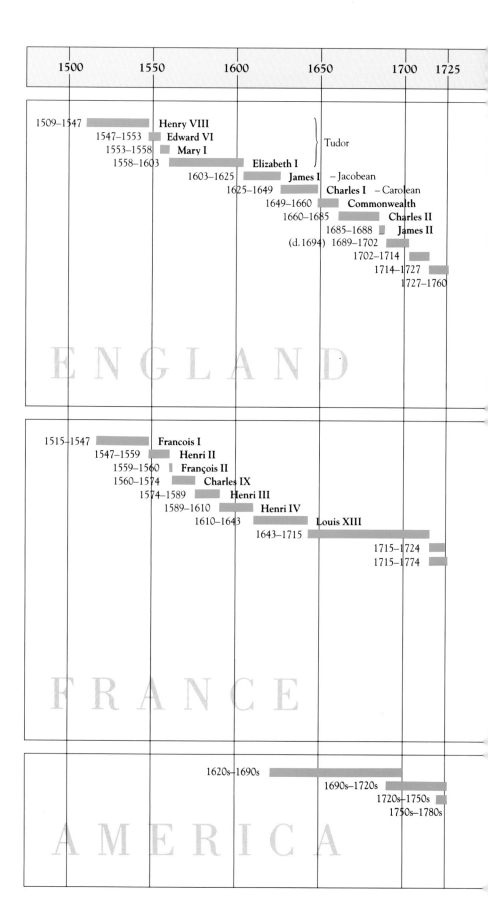

ENGLAND

| 1500 | 1550 | 1600 | 1650 | 1700 | 1725 |

1509–1547 Henry VIII
1547–1553 Edward VI
1553–1558 Mary I
1558–1603 Elizabeth I
} Tudor
1603–1625 James I – Jacobean
1625–1649 Charles I – Carolean
1649–1660 Commonwealth
1660–1685 Charles II
1685–1688 James II
(d.1694) 1689–1702
1702–1714
1714–1727
1727–1760

FRANCE

1515–1547 Francois I
1547–1559 Henri II
1559–1560 François II
1560–1574 Charles IX
1574–1589 Henri III
1589–1610 Henri IV
1610–1643 Louis XIII
1643–1715 Louis XIII
1715–1724
1715–1774

AMERICA

1620s–1690s
1690s–1720s
1720s–1750s
1750s–1780s

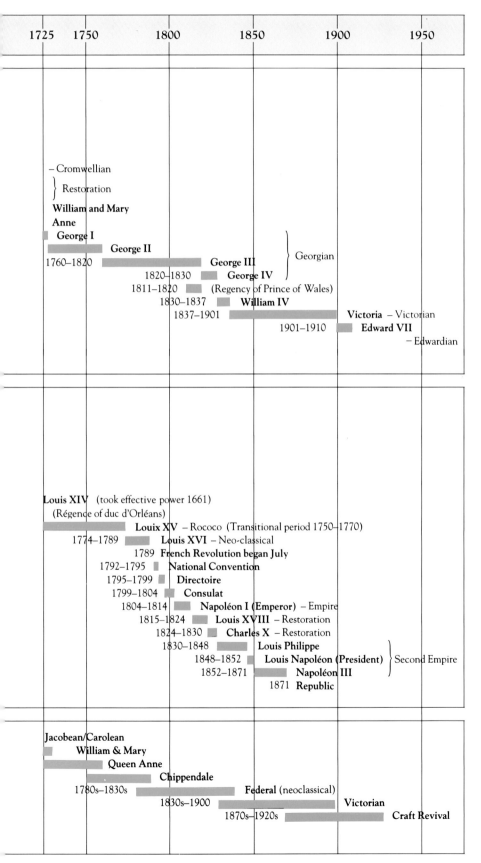

1725	1750	1800	1850	1900	1950

– Cromwellian

} Restoration

William and Mary

Anne

George I

George II

1760–1820

George III
1820–1830 **George IV**
1811–1820 (Regency of Prince of Wales)
1830–1837 **William IV**
1837–1901 **Victoria** – Victorian
1901–1910 **Edward VII**
– Edwardian

} Georgian

Louis XIV (took effective power 1661)
(Régence of duc d'Orléans)
Louix XV – Rococo (Transitional period 1750–1770)
1774–1789 **Louis XVI** – Neo-classical
1789 French Revolution began July
1792–1795 **National Convention**
1795–1799 **Directoire**
1799–1804 **Consulat**
1804–1814 **Napoléon I (Emperor)** – Empire
1815–1824 **Louis XVIII** – Restoration
1824–1830 **Charles X** – Restoration
1830–1848 **Louis Philippe**
1848–1852 **Louis Napoléon (President)**
1852–1871 **Napoléon III**
1871 **Republic**

} Second Empire

Jacobean/Carolean
William & Mary
Queen Anne
Chippendale
1780s–1830s **Federal** (neoclassical)
1830s–1900 **Victorian**
1870s–1920s **Craft Revival**

Cabinetmakers' pattern books and other influential publications

Listed here is a selection of books influential both on the furniture makers and designers of their times and on furniture historians.

Stalker and Parker, **Treatise of Japanning and Varnishing**, 1688

Thomas Chippendale, **Gentleman and Cabinet-Maker's Director**, 1754 (2nd edition 1755; 3rd edition 1762)

Ince and Mayhew, **Universal System of Household Furniture**, 1759–1762

Robert Manwaring, **Cabinet and Chair-Maker's Real Friend and Companion** 1765

Robert and James Adam, **Works in Architecture**, 1773–1778 (2nd volume 1779; 3rd volume 1822)

George Hepplewhite, **Cabinet-Maker and Upholsterer's Guide**, 1788

Thomas Shearer, Hepplewhite and others, **Cabinet-Maker's London Book of Prices**, 1788

Thomas Sheraton, **Cabinet-Maker and Upholsterer's Drawing-Book**, 1791–1794

Percier and Fontaine, **Receuil des décorations intérieurs**, 1801 (2nd edition 1812)

Thomas Sheraton, **Cabinet Dictionary**, 1803

Thomas Hope, **Household Furniture and Interior Decoration**, 1807

George Smith, **Collection of Designs for Household Furniture and Interior Decoration**, 1808

Collection of Ornamental Designs after the Antique, 1812

Cabinet Maker and Upholsterer's Guide, 1826

John C. Loudon, **Encyclopaedia of Cottage, Farm and Villa Furniture**, 1833

Augustus W.N. Pugin, **Gothic Furniture in the style of the 15th century**, 1835

The True Principle of Pointed or Christian Architecture, 1841

Bruce Talbert, **Gothic Forms Applied to Furniture**, 1867

Charles Eastlake, **Hints on Household Taste**, 1868

acanthus – A classical ornamental device based on the prickly, indented leaves of the acanthus plant, used especially in the capitals of Corinthian and Composite columns.

Adirondack Rustic/Hickory – Summer furniture made of hickory at several factories in Indiana between 1898 and 1940. Hickory saplings were bent into shape on metal frames, and the inner bark was cut into strips for the woven sections.

anthemion – A classical ornament consisting of a band of alternating floral forms based on the honeysuckle flower. A single motif based on the honeysuckle is also called an anthemion.

apron – An ornamental projection below a rail, often shaped and carved.

Art Deco – Term deriving from the *Exposition des Arts Décoratifs et Industriels Modernes* held in Paris in 1925. It is generally used today to describe progressive furniture from c1910 to 1940, from luxurious and expensive Parisian pieces to Modernist examples created by industrial designers.

Art Nouveau – French term for essentially curvilinear style which was often asymmetrical and derived from organic forms, especially stems and leaves. Developed in the late 19th century, its influence extended into the 1920s. Called *Jugendstil* in Germany and *Stile Liberty* in Italy.

Arts & Crafts Movement – Design movement of the second half of the 19th century, whose English and American exponents attempted to create beautiful, well-designed furnishings which would improve the quality of life through their daily use.

ball-and-claw foot – A foot in the form of a claw clutching a ball, often used in conjunction with a cabriole leg and popular in England and America in the 18th century.

baluster (banister) – A short supporting column, bulbous near the base, used in series to form a balustrade.

banding – Veneer was often used in bands to form decorative borders to the main surface. Crossbanding was cut across the grain, while feather or herringbone banding was cut with the grain at an angle so that two strips laid side by side resembled a feather.

banister – See baluster.

Baroque – A decorative style which originated in Italy and reached its height in the 17th century, characterized by heavy and exuberant forms. Its influence varied from country to country but Baroque furniture tends to be sculptural and often architectural in form and is frequently gilded, with human figures, scrolls and shells much in evidence.

Bauhaus – German design school established in 1919 under the direction of Walter Gropius in Weimar. At first, artist/craftsman pieces were made, but after the move to Dessau in 1925 the main interest was in the area of good industrial design with an emphasis on functionalism.

bentwood – Wood which is bent by steam or boiling water in special moulds. First developed in Austria in the 1830s by Michael Thonet, whose Vienna factory employed mainly beech. Popular for light sofas or chaises longues with wicker seats and backs.

Biedermeier – A German term used to denote both the period 1815–1848 and the decorative style popular in Germany, Austria and Scandinavia from the 1820s to the 1840s, which was characterized by solid, unpretentious furniture in light-coloured woods. Biedermeier was a newspaper caricature symbolizing the uncultured bourgeoisie.

bird's-eye maple – Maple with a regular burr pattern resembling a bird's eye; very popular in the 19th century.

blind fret – A cut-work design set against a flat background.

bolster – A long cushion. Can be rectangular or cylindrical, with the latter versions often used in pairs.

boulle – Elaborate marquetry of brass, tortoiseshell and other substances, introduced to France by André-Charles Boulle (1642–1732).

burl – The American term for burr.

burr – See veneer.

C-scroll – A scroll in the shape of a letter C, a favourite Rococo motif.

cabochon – An oval or round boss used decoratively, usually in conjunction with other motifs.

cabriole leg – A sinuous tapering leg, curving outwards at the knee, in towards the ankle and out again at the foot.

canapé – A French sofa with arms.

canted – When legs or projected members are set at an angle to the corner of a piece they are known as canted legs or canted corners.

capital – The head of a column, usually decorated according to the different architectural orders, ie, Doric (plain disc-like capital), Ionic (with four scroll corners), Corinthian (decorated with bands of acanthus leaves), Composite (a combination of Ionic and Corinthian).

cartouche – An ornamental panel, often a stylized shield, which is decorative itself but can also carry an inscription, a monogram or a crest.

cassapanca – Italian settle with arms and back. The finest specimens are from the late 16th century.

cassone – An Italian form of low chest, richly carved and made as a formal piece of furniture.

castors – Small swivelling wheels attached to the bottom of furniture, to make it easier to move the piece.

chair-back sofa – A sofa whose back rest gives the appearance of two to four chairs set side by side.

chaise longue – French term for a long, upholstered seat with a back rest, intended for only one person to recline on.

chamfer – A narrow flat surface formed by cutting away the apex of an angle between two surfaces, thus removing the sharp edge. Hence chamfered leg, chamfered stretcher etc.

Chesterfield – An upholstered sofa with the arms and back forming a low, unbroken line. Deeply padded and often buttoned.

chinoiserie – A Western imitation of Chinese decoration, usually more fanciful than accurate and frequently used to give an exotic touch to a basically European design.

chintz – Cotton or calico with a printed pattern which is sometimes glazed. First versions exported from India in the 17th century.

cipher – A monogram or symbol.

Classical – Term usually referring to the superb work of Greece and Rome, which was controlled by rules such as the Five Orders of Architecture.

classicism – Various interpretations of the Classical tradition.

confident – A sofa with attached chairs set at either end; sometimes two sofas set back to back with a chair set between at either end.

Consulate – The period of government in France between 1799 and 1804.

conversation – A sofa with seats arranged back to back or facing, so that the sitters can converse discreetly. In some Victorian pattern-books, these are described as ottomans.

cornucopia – A horn of plenty, used decoratively as a shell-like horn overflowing with fruit.

cresting – The carved ornament on the top rail of a chair-back.

cresting rail – See top rail.

cretonne – Strong, unglazed cotton with a printed pattern.

crinoline stretcher – An inward-curving stretcher designed to accommodate a full skirt.

crossbanding – See banding.

crosspiece – A member that stretches across a piece of furniture.

cross-stretcher – A stretcher that runs across a piece of furniture; sometimes decorated.

day-bed – A sofa for one person to recline on during the day, sometimes for the formal reception of visitors.

demilune – Half-moon shape.

dowelled – Linked with a headless pin of wood or metal.

drop-in seat – A removable upholstered or caned seat which rests on blocks inside the seat rails of a chair.

ébéniste – A French term for a cabinetmaker, a specialist in veneered furniture, as distinct from a *menuisier* or joiner who specialized in carved pieces like chairs or beds. A *maître* of the Paris furniture makers' guild (*Corporation des menuisiers-ébénistes*) was not bound to specialize, but the distinction was generally observed until the end of the 18th century.

estampille – The stamp with the name and initials of a *maître ébéniste* which was obligatory on French furniture from about 1750 until the Revolution. The mark was struck with a cold punch rather than branded, although delicate pieces could be signed in ink. Long names were sometimes shortened, as in BVRB for Bernard van Risenburgh, and the marks were usually in an inconspicuous place, often accompanied by the monogram of the *Corporation des Jurés Menuisiers-Ébénistes* – JME conjoined – a quality control mark. Furniture made for the crown did not have to be stamped and royal craftsmen were exempt.

escutcheon – Shield-shaped mounts or an armorial shield used as the centre ornament of a pediment.

fauteuil – A French upholstered chair with open arms, sometimes with armrests. Term used from the late 17th century.

festoon – A neo-Classical decorative motif in the form of a looped garland of flowers, fruit and foliage.

figure – The natural grain patterns of a veneer are known as figuring.

finial – An ornamental projection from the top of a piece of furniture, often a knob, ball, acorn, urn or flame.

fluting – Decorative in the form of shallow, parallel grooves, especially on columns and pilasters or on the legs of furniture.

fretwork – Carved geometrical patterns, either in relief or pierced, or sawn with a fretsaw.

frieze – A band of decoration usually found on the top rail of a sofa.

gadroon – A form of decorative edging usually in the form of a series of convex curved lobes or repeated spiral ribs resembling ropetwist.

gesso – A mixture of powdered chalk and size.

gilding – The application of gold to the surface of another material. Bronze mounts were frequently gilded to prevent tarnishing, especially in France. Wood was also gilded for decorative effect.

gilt – See gilding.

gimp – Simple silk or cotton braid used for concealment of joins.

Gothic – A decorative style based on the pointed arches, cluster columns, spires and other elements of late medieval architecture. Gothic revivals have influenced furniture design at several periods, particularly in Britain in the mid-18th century and again in the mid-19th century.

gros-point – French term for stitched work on canvas. The regular stitches are laid over two threads so that the effect is coarser than petit-point.

hump-back – A sofa with a sudden sweeping curve.

inlay – Although it is often used to mean marquetry, inlay strictly refers to decorative materials like ivory or ebony set into the surface of solid wood, unlike veneer which covers the whole surface.

japanning – The term used in America and Britain for techniques imitating the Oriental lacquerwork which began to arrive in Europe via the Dutch East India Company in the 17th century.

joinery – Joined furniture is formed of vertical and horizontal members, united by mortice and tenon joints and supporting panels.

lancet – An arch with a pointed top.

latticework – Pattern or structure of crossed regular lines.

lion-paw foot – Furniture foot carved in the form of a lion's paw.

lit de repos – French form of day-bed introduced in the early 17th century; intended for one person.

love seat – A small sofa introduced in the mid-17th century. Sometimes called a 'courting chair', as two people needed to sit very closely on it.

maître – A mastercraftsman under the Paris guild system, who was entitled to own a workshop and stamp his pieces, having served an apprenticeship and paid the necessary fees. See *estampille*.

marquetry – The use of veneers (woods of different colours, bone, ivory, mother-of-pearl, tortoiseshell, etc.) to form decorative designs like scrolls, flowers and landscapes. Abstract geometrical patterns formed in the same manner are known as parquetry.

member – Any of the structural components (rails, uprights, stretchers etc.) of a piece of joined furniture.

menuisier – See *ébéniste*.

méridienne – An 18th-century French form of day-bed, curving up at one or both ends to form scrolls.

mitred – Joint wherein the two pieces connect after they are cut at half the angle of the joint, eg, 45° for a right angle.

modular seating – Type of seating wherein complementary units, built to standard sizes, can be linked or placed against one another to form a variety of arrangements.

monopodium – Greek-derived term for a single foot, eg, as in a table which stands on a single column.

moquette – Fabric with a wool pile. Some varieties are cut in imitation of cut silk velvet.

moulding – A length of wood or other material applied to the surface of a piece of furniture. The shaped section of a moulding is usually made up from a number of curves, and there are various standard types (astragal, ogee, cavetto, ovolo) mostly of architectural origin.

mounts – Decorative motifs, usually of brass or gilt-bronze, fixed to cabinetwork and sometimes seat furniture.

neo-Classicism – The predominant decorative style of the second half of the 18th century. Based on the restrained use of Greek and Roman architectural form and ornament, it is characterized by a sober, rectilinear emphasis which was a conscious reaction to the exuberance of the Rococo.

ogee arch – Slender, S-shaped line with two moulded curves which meet at the apex.

ormolu – Gilt bronze. A term derived from the French *or moulu* (literally ground gold).

out-scrolled – Curving outwards in a nearly horizontal plane.

outward-splayed – At a significant angle from perpendicular, the distance at the bottom between the legs being greater than that at the top.

overstuffed – Type of furniture whose stuffing and upholstery completely covers the frame.

panel – A flat surface supported by rails and stiles in joined furniture.

parcel gilt – Gilded in part only.

parquetry – See marquetry.

patera – A neo-Classical decorative motif, either oval or round, resembling a stylized flower or rosette.

petit-point – French term for embroidery in small stitches on canvas, comprising at least 15 stitches to the inch.

pierced – Carved ornament is described as pierced when the decoration is cut right through the piece, as in fretwork.

pilaster – A shallow column attached to a piece of furniture.

punchwork – Decoration achieved by the use of punches struck by a hammer.

putto (pl. putti) – A naked infant, often winged, used as a decorative motif. Also referred to as a cherub, a cupid or an amoretto.

rail – A horizontal member used in the construction of joined furniture.

ratchet – A toothed wheel which engages with a catch to prevent motion in one direction, while allowing it in the other.

reeding – Decoration in the form of parallel ribbing, especially on columns and pilasters or on the legs of furniture.

Régence – Regency of the Duc d'Orléans in France (1715–24).

Renaissance – The rebirth of ancient Roman values in the arts which began in Italy in the 14th century and gradually replaced the Gothic style in most of Europe during the following two and a half centuries. Renaissance designers were inspired by the sculpture and architectural remains of the ancient world and their furniture reflects this in the profusion of carved ornament.

repoussé work – A form of embossed decoration produced by hammering sheet metal from the underside.

ribbon-back – Wood carved in imitation of ribbons and bows on chair and sofa backs. A style popularized by Chippendale.

Rococo – A decorative style which spread from France during the first half of the 18th century, characterized by delicate curved outlines, C-scrolls, fantastic shell and rock forms and a tendency towards asymmetry in ornamental details.

roundel – A circular form of ornament.

sabre leg – A furniture leg which is curved and tapered like a cavalry sabre.

salon – A French reception room.

saloon – Large, formal reception room in a stately British home.

scroll couch – A couch with a scrolled end.

seat rail – The horizontal framework which supports the seat of a joined chair.

serpentine – In the form of an undulating curve, convex at the centre and concave on each side.

settee – An upholstered sofa.

settle – A wooden bench-like seat with a back and arms; sometimes has a box base for storage.

show-wood – Wood which is revealed on a piece of furniture; often polished.

side rail – Wooden connecting struts at the sides of chairs or sofas.

spindle – A slim, turned rod frequently used as an upright in chair backs.

splat – The central upright member of a chair back which joins the seat to the top rail.

spoon back – The back of a chair or sofa which is curved like a spoon.

squab cushion – A stuffed cushion with straight sides. Originally used in 17th-century day-beds, it is primarily connected today with modular seating, which uses rubber or foam cushions.

square-section leg – A leg which would be square if cut at right-angles, but which may also be tapering or shaped in some other way.

stile – A vertical member used in the construction of joined furniture.

strapwork – A form of decoration particularly popular in Northern Europe in the 16th and 17th centuries, resembling interlaced, pierced and scrolled bands of leather.

stretcher – A horizontal crosspiece used to join and strengthen the legs of a piece of furniture.

stringing – Thin strips of wood or metal inlay used to decorate furniture.

strung border – A border decorated with stringing.

stuff-over – A term used when the upholstery of a chair covers the framework rather than being a panel within it. Hence stuff-over seat.

swag – A decorative motif in the form of a loop of cloth and similar to a festoon.

tempera – Powder colour mixed with thinned egg yolk. The paint work dries quickly and gives a tough surface.

tête-à-tête – Various constructions wherein the seats are angled towards one another. See *confident*.

top rail – The topmost horizontal member which joins the uprights of a chair back. Also known as a yoke rail or a cresting rail.

tracery – Ornamental openwork.

turned leg – A leg shaped on a lathe, usually circular in section and mainly fashionable before the beginning of the 18th century. Turned legs are found in many traditional patterns, e.g. bobbin – a series of small bulbs or bobbins; bobbin and ring – small bulbs interspaced by rings; bulb – a large bulbous swelling of elongated melon form, often carved and used with a base and capital to form a leg; barley-sugar or barley-twist – a double spiral resembling a barleysugar sweet; vase – in the shape of a vase, usually slim at the base and gradually increasing in diameter towards the top; baluster – in the shape of a baluster, bulbous at the base and slim towards the top.

under-frame – The supporting structure of a piece of furniture, including legs, stretchers and any other braces.

uprights – The vertical parts of a chair back, formed as continuations of the rear legs.

veneer – A very thin sheet, usually of wood, applied to the surface of a piece of furniture. Veneers cut from knotty areas of the tree are particularly decorative and known as burrs, hence burr walnut.

Vitruvian scroll – Formal decoration resembling waves in S shapes; used especially on Classical furniture, often as a frieze ornament. Also known as Greek wave pattern.

yoke rail – See top rail.

A DOUBLE CHAIR-BACK SOFA
EXHIBITED AT THE 1851 GREAT EXHIBITION, LONDON

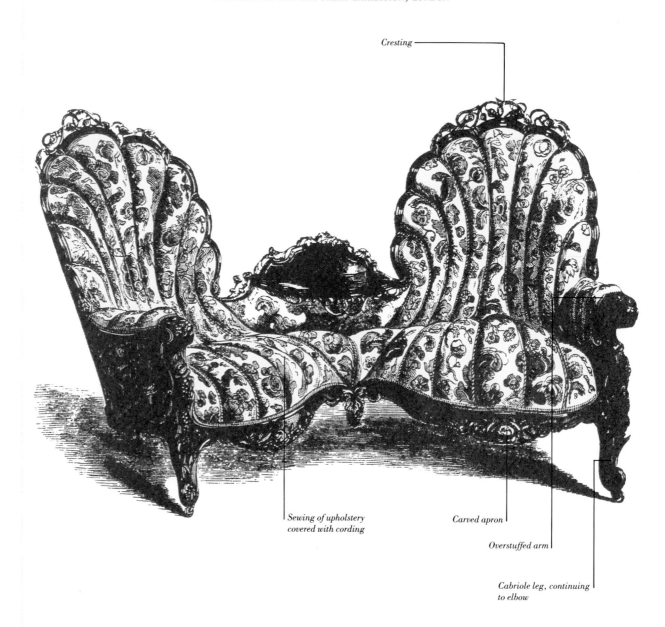

Cresting

Sewing of upholstery
covered with cording

Carved apron

Overstuffed arm

Cabriole leg, continuing
to elbow

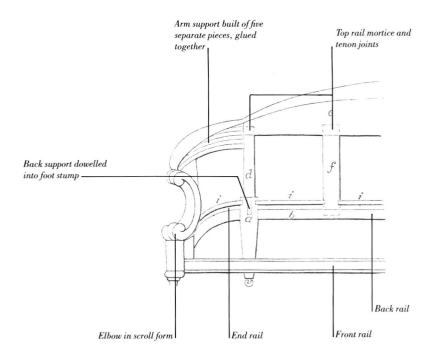

*Arm support built of five
separate pieces, glued
together*

*Top rail mortice and
tenon joints*

*Back support dowelled
into foot stump*

Elbow in scroll form

End rail

Front rail

Back rail

DIAGRAMS SHOWING CONSTRUCTION TECHNIQUES, FROM
THE CABINETMAKER'S ASSISTANT,
PUBLISHED IN 1853

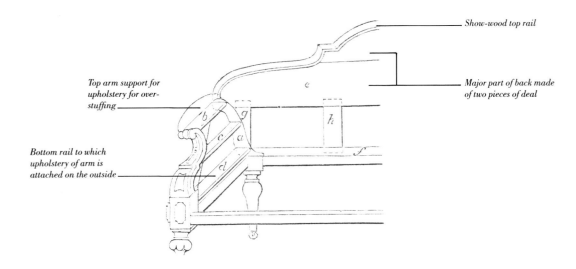

*Top arm support for
upholstery for over-
stuffing*

*Bottom rail to which
upholstery of arm is
attached on the outside*

Show-wood top rail

*Major part of back made
of two pieces of deal*

Figures in *italics* refer to relevant captions.

A
Aalto, Alvar 87
Adam, Robert 17, *34, 40, 42, 44*
Adirondack Rustic form 49, *124*
aluminium sofas *116*
American sofas 7
  19th century 49, *54, 57*
  Empire style (c1815) *56*
  Federal style (1799–1830) *50, 52*
  Rococo Revival 69, *70*
  20th century 87, 88, *92, 94, 106, 108, 110, 116*
  French and Italian influence 17
'Angaraib' chaise longue *118*
animal feet 9, 10, 18, *50, 56, 67, 72*
  ball-and-claw 20, *23, 61, 72*
animal-skin covers 87
  leather *90, 92, 110, 112, 117*
arms, distinctive *42, 46, 60, 87, 88, 90, 98, 101*
Art Deco 92, *101, 102, 103, 104,* 124
Art Nouveau sofas 84, 87, 88, 90, 124
Arts and Crafts Movement style 49, 72, 84, 92, 94, 124
Aubusson tapestry *74*
Austrian sofa: Hoffman *92*

B
Baillie Scott, Hugh Mackay 87, 94
ball-and-claw feet 20, *23, 61, 72,* 124
bamboo, simulated *53*
banquette *88*
Baroque 124
Bauhaus 87, *106, 110,* 124
bay windows, curved sofa *74*
Bell, Vanessa *106*
Belter, John Henry 49, 69, *70*
benches, wooden *12, 20, 94*
bentwood sofas 92, 124
Biedermeier style 60, *61,* 124
bird's-eye maple sofa *45,* 124
Blacker House, Pasadena *92*
Boulle, André-Charles: Revival 68, *72*
'Boxing Gloves' chaises longues *110*
brass inlay *60, 68*
Breuer, Marcel 87, *106*
British Empire Exhibition (1924) *100*
British sofas 7
  French and Italian influence 17
  see also George I *etc*
Broecke, Floris van den *110, 112, 118*
Bugatti, Carlo *88*
built-in sofas 87, *90, 94, 100*
Bullock, George *54*

C
canapés *18, 20, 22, 36, 38, 40, 42,* 124
canework *55, 56, 58*
carving, distinctive *64, 69*
cassapanca 9, 124
castors *60,* 124
chair-back sofas, 124
  double *20, 24, 28, 32*
  four-seater (or quadruple) *53, 55, 58*
  triple *24, 31, 32, 54, 58, 68, 88*
'Chairpiece I' *110*
'chaise longue' 7
chaises longues 49, *50, 60, 67, 101, 104, 106, 110, 117, 118,* 124
  Victorian *63, 66, 67, 75*
  see also day-beds
'Chesterfield' 7
Chesterfields 7, *88, 90, 97, 98, 112,* 124
Chinese style *53, 58, 100*
  Chippendale 17, *29*
chintz 87, 124
Chippendale, Thomas 17, 28, *29, 30, 32*
chrome sofas 87
City Cabinet Works, Moorgate *104*

'Civitas' *112*
Coard, Marcel *101*
confidents 17, *124*
'conversation' sofas *78, 79,* 124
convertible sofas 17, *88, 98, 104, 112*
corners,
  corner sofa *34*
  'Cosy Corners' 49
  sofas shaped around corners 49, *114*
cottage, Tudor-style *100*
'couch' 7
Craftsman Workshops, NY, and Gustave Stickley 49, *94*
curved sofas *74*
  see also corners
cushions 87, *95, 96, 97*

D
Dali, Salvador: 'Mae West Hot Lips Sofa' *106*
Danish furniture: Kastholm *117*
d'Arcy, William Knox *84*
'day-bed' 7
day-beds 124
  classical 9
  English *14, 72*
  French *30, 52, 61*
  see also chaises longues
De Sede chaises longues *110*
deep-buttoning *75, 79*
Dillon, Jane *112*
'divan' 7
Dufrêne, Maurice *102*
Dufresne, Charles *102*
Dunand, Jean *101*
Dutch Sofas *20, 46*

E
Eames, Charles 87, *110, 116*
Eastlake, Charles Lock 87
'Eastside' sofa *114*
ebonized-wood sofas *26, 54, 55, 68*
Edwardian sofas 88, *90, 91, 93*
Egyptian sofas and day-beds 9, *10, 17*
Egyptian style 49
Empire style, 20th century *103*
Empire-style *56*
English sofas 7, 17
  William & Mary *12, 84*
  see also George I *etc*
exhibitions, international 49
  Paris (1825) *101, 102*

F
'Fakir's Divan' *116*
feather-filled cushions 87, *96, 97*
Finland: Alvar Aalto 87
Flemish sofas *12*
foam padding 87, *104*
Foliot, Nicolas-Quinibert and Foliot family *31*
Follot, Paul *103*
'French chairs' (of Chippendale) *32*
French guilds 30, *31*
French sofas 7, 9, *19*
  19th century *52, 61, 62, 67, 68, 72*
  20th century *101, 102, 103*
  canapés *18, 20, 22, 31*
  Consulate period (1799–804) *50*
  identification, 30
  influence 17, *24, 28, 46, 52, 63, 66, 80, 84*
  'sociables' *78*
  see also Louis XV sofas *etc*
Furniture Designers, London *112*

G
Galeries Lafayette *102*
George I sofas *18, 20*
George II sofas *22, 23, 24, 26, 28, 29, 30*
George II style, 19th century *72*
George III sofas *31, 32, 34, 36, 39, 40, 42, 44, 46*

George III style, 20th century *88*
German sofas 7, *32, 38, 44, 45*
  19th century 49, *63, 69*
    Biedermeier style *60*
  20th century 87, *90, 95, 106*
  French influence 17, *63*
gilt-wood sofas,
  pre-1700 *14*
  18th century 9, *18, 20, 24, 26, 30, 36, 38, 40, 42, 44*
  19th century *53, 56, 57, 62, 74, 78, 80, 82, 84*
  20th century *96, 102, 103*
Glasgow School (Mackintosh) 90, *93*
glass chaises longues *118*
Gobelins tapestries *40*
Goodison, Benjamin *72*
Gordon Russell Design Group *112, 114*
Gothic revival 49, *54, 58,* 124
Graaf, Eric de *117*
Grant, Duncan *106*
'Great Couches' 9
Great Exhibition, London (1851) 49, *76*
Greek sofas 9, 17
  see also neo-Classical sofas
Greene, Charles and Henry 92
Gropius, Walter 87
Grosfield House, NY: exhibition *106*
guilds 30, *31*

H
half-round sofas *74*
Hampton & Sons *74, 75, 76, 78, 79*
Heal & Son, London 87, *95, 97*
Heal, Ambrose Jr *95, 97*
Hepplewhite, George, style *38*
Herman Miller, Inc *108, 110*
High Victorian overstuffed effect 49
Hill House, Dunbartonshire *90*
Hoffman, Josef *92*
Hollywood influence *101*
Hope, Thomas 49, *50*
hump-back settee *32,* 125

I
identification,
  dating *62*
  labels and marks, French stamped with maker's name 17, 30
  reproductions 7
imitations 7, 32, 49, 84
Indian sofas *14,* 49
inlay 9, *50, 54, 60,* 125
  Boulle (tortoiseshell, wood and brass) 68, *72*
  brass *60*
iron-framed sofa *79*
Isokon company, London *106*
Italian sofas 9
  18th century *24, 32, 36*
  20th century *88, 110, 114*
  influence 17

J
Jack, George *84*
Jackson, Lorin *106*
Jacob Frères *50*
Jacob, Georges *36, 38*
Jacobean style 49x
Japanese craftsmen 49x
Japanese influence 49, *92, 101, 117*
Joel, Betty *104*

K
Kastholm, Jørgen *117*
Kent, William 17, *22, 26*
'kitsch' *108*
Knole sofas 7, 9, *96*
Knoll company *110*

L
La Maîtrise 102
lacquered sofas 101
laminated materials 49, 69, 70, 87, 104, 106
Lane, Danny 116, 118
Le Corbusier 87
leather covers 90, 92, 110, 112, 117
Leeds, Duke of 14
Legrain, Pierre 101
Lethaby, W. R. 84
Linnell, John 34, 44
lion, winged: feet 67
lion-paw feet 9, 10, 56, 72, 124
lips: 'Mae West Hot Lips Sofa' 106
lits-de-repos 9, 17, 125
'Longford' range 114
loose covers 54, 87, 98
Louis XV sofas 19, 20, 22, 30
Louis XV style, revivals 62, 80, 96
Louis XVI sofas 31, 36, 38, 40
Louis XVI style (19th century revival) 62, 74, 82
love seats 10, 18, 70, 125
Lutyens, Sir Edwin 104

M
McIntyre, Samuel 52
Mackintosh, Charles Rennie, and Glasgow School 84, 87, 90, 93
'Mae West Hot Lips Sofa' 106
mahogany 17, 34, 42, 46, 55
Mare, André 102
marquetry 9, 46, 125
    Boulle 68, 72
'Marshmallow' sofa 108
mass market, mass production 49, 84, 87, 95, 103, 108, 110, 116
medallion decorations 36, 100
Memphis (Milanese group) 114
meridienne (French day-bed) 61, 125
metal 87, 88
Midland Furniture Galleries, Southampton Row, London 103
Moderne style 102, 103, 104, 106
modular design 87, 112, 114, 116
Moorish styles 88
    ottomans 78
Morris, William 49, 72, 84, 87, 94
Morton, Graham 84
Moser, Koloman 92
Mr Freedom (London shop) 108

N
needlework upholstery 17, 18, 22, 26, 36, 72, 84
    see also tapestry upholstery
Nelson, George 108
neo-Classical sofas 125
    18th century 17, 34, 36, 38, 46
    19th century 49, 50, 56, 57

O
'Op Art' 108
oriental styles 88
    see also Chinese; Japanese
ormolu decoration 52, 55, 67, 68, 72, 125
Osterley Park, Middlesex 44
ottomans 78
'Out of Babylon' 118
oval backs, padded 62X

P
painted sofas 20, 22, 38, 40, 42, 44
    19th century 54, 57
    20th century 88, 93, 106
Palais Stoclet, Brussels 92
Palazzo Rezzonico, Venice, sofa 24
papier-mâché sofas 49
parcel-gilt sofas 32, 38, 54, 55, 58, 72, 125
pattern-books 17, 121
Perriand, Charlotte 87

Phyfe, Duncan 57
plastic furniture 106, 110, 116
plastic preformed cushions 87
Plexiglas furniture 106
Pop Art sofas 108
public house settles 82
Pugin, Augustus Welby 49, 58

Q
Queen Anne sofas 18, 49
Queen Anne style (20th century) 90, 91

R
Régence sofas 18, 19
Regency period 53, 54, 55, 57, 58, 60, 125
    Victorian revival 76
Renaissance-Revival sofas 66
reproduction pieces 7, 49, 84, 87, 88, 91, 104
    public house settles 82
ribbon-back carving 28, 125
Rococo Revival 49, 69, 70
Rococo sofas 17, 18, 32, 34, 125
Rohm & Haas Co Inc 106
Roman sofas 9, 10
    see also neo-Classical sofas
rush seating 72
Ruskin, John 49
Russell, Gordon 112, 114
Russian sofas 17, 50

S
Scott, Mackay Hugh Baillie 87, 94
Scottish sofas 84, 87, 90
'Segmenta' range 114
'settee' 7
settees 14, 15
    18th century 36
    double-ended 63
'settle' 7
settles 29, 39, 42, 72, 84, 125
    19th century bentwood 49
    20th century 92, 94, 100, 101
    double chair-back 20
    triple chair-back 31, 32, 88
    Victorian public house 82
Shaker furniture 94
Sheraton, Thomas 17, 53
show-wood 7, 17, 49, 125
silk trimmings 75
silk upholstery fabric 42, 78, 80
smoking room: lacquered settle 101
'sociable' (or 'conversation') sofas 78, 79
'sofa' 7
'Soft Pad' sofas 116
Sottsass, Ettore 114
spoon-back form 49, 125
sprung seats 7, 49, 63, 70, 87, 88, 90, 98
Stanmore Hall, Middlesex 84
stapled upholstery 87
steel sofas 87, 104, 106
Stickley, Gustav, and Craftsman Workshops, NY 49, 94
storage provision in sofas 92, 94, 101, 108
striped fabric, deep-buttoned 75
Studio Alchymia 114
Süe, Louis 102
synthetic materials 87, 106, 110, 116

T
tapestry upholstery 22, 26, 40, 46, 74, 80, 84, 93, 102, 103
Temple Newsam House, Leeds 14
tête-à-tête 17, 125
Thonet, Michael 49
three-piece suites 98
throne, Indian 14
Tilliard, Jean-Baptiste 30
tin-lined furniture 108
tortoiseshell inlay 68

tree-branch chaise longue 118
trimmings, 20th century 87, 98
trimmings (braids, fringes, tassels) 7, 9, 54, 76, 87
    distinctive pieces 75, 78, 79, 88
Tudor (cottage) style 100

U
unit sealing 87
upholstery 9, 39, 46, 63, 79
    20th century 87, 93, 116
    custom-woven 79, 106
    deep-buttoned striped fabric 75
    distinctive 14, 40, 44, 56, 70, 106, 108
    Hamptons upholstery department 74, 76
    loose covers 54, 87, 98
    mass produced sofas 49
    Morris fabric 'Flower Garden' 84
    of needlework 17, 18, 19, 22, 36, 72
    replacement 46, 49, 60x, 62, 63, 76, 78
    replacement, high cost 76, 79
    sofas of particular interest, needlework 22
    squab cushions 38
    stapled 87
upholstery fabrics 7, 23, 26, 42, 68, 78, 80
    20th century 87, 88
    leather 90, 92, 110, 112, 117
    20th century colours and patterns 87, 95, 98
    synthetic 87, 103
    see also tapestry upholstery
upholstery fillings, stuffings 12, 30, 49
    20th century, feathers 87, 96, 97
    foam 87, 104

V
veneers 9, 125
Vernaschi, Minoc 114
Victorian Cabinetmaker's Assistant 64
Victorian sofas 61, 62, 63, 64, 67, 68, 70, 72, 74–84, 88
    reaction against 84, 93
    Renaissance-Revival 66
'Vis-à-Vis' sofa 118
Voysey, C.F.A. 87, 90

W
'Westbury' 112
Wheeler, Peter 112
White, J. P. 94
Wiener Werkstätte 92
Wilder, Billy 110
William & Mary sofas 12, 84
window-seat sofas 100
windows, curved sofa for bay windows 74
Windsor style 88
woods 10, 17, 26, 38, 45
    elm and yew Windsor settles 88
    laminated 87, 104, 106
    laminated and steam-moulded 49, 69, 70
    mahogany 17, 34, 38, 42, 46, 55
    for marquetry, veneers and inlay 46, 66, 68
    oak 54
    oak benches and settles 29, 49, 94
    pine 26, 44
    rosewood 58, 60, 69
    selected by customer for the construction 76
    to simulate bamboo (faux-bamboo) 53
woods and woodwork, machine-made decorations 76
World War I: influence 87
World War II: influence 87

Z
Ziehmer, Kurt 112